SMALL CHANGE

"Helping people help themselves" is the motto of microcredit. It may not be the complete answer to the problem of world poverty, but it is the only approach that has resulted in proliferating successes in many parts of Asia, Africa and South America.

The metaphor for development co-operation is catching fish. First the rich countries send fish to the poor. Then they send fishing poles so the poor themselves can fish for their own sustenance. Next, the poor borrow money to buy the fishing poles. Finally they pay off their loans. This small-scale development aid doesn't cost any money, but it is effective. And the beauty of it is that the capital for procuring the credit doesn't have to come from the West.

– Jurriaan Kamp

Jurriaan Kamp

Small Change

How $50 Can Change the World

Translated by Nancy Forest-Flier

COSIMO ON DEMAND

NEW YORK

Small Change
Copyright © 2003 Jurriaan Kamp
Dutch rights Lemniscaat b.v., Rotterdam, 2003

ISBN: 1596057874

Copyright © Cover photo: Maartje Geels/Hollandse Hoogte

Cosimo
P.O. Box 416
Old Chelsea Station
New York, NY 10113-0416

Or visit our Web site at www.cosimobooks.com

Library of Congress Cataloging-in-Publication Data
A catalog record for this book is available from the Library of Congress

Contents

For Benjamin Byarugaba (Masindi, Uganda), Udaia Kumar (Hyderabad, India), Vijay Mahajan (Hyderabad, India), Kimanthi Mutua (Nairobi, Kenya) and Pilar Ramirez (La Paz, Bolivia), big entrepreneurs in small change.

And for the whistling shoeshine boy of about 7 who polished my shoes at 10 o'clock at night in La Paz. I don't know his name, but his beaming smile and enthusiasm are etched in my memory. One day he'll be a successful job maker. I'm sure of it.

Prologue

According to the Greek historian Herodotus, the walls of ancient Babylon were among the wonders of the world. Herodotus writes that the walls were 50 metres high and more than 80 kilometres long. A chariot pulled by a team of four horses could run along the top. Apparently this description was a bit of an exaggeration. Whether Herodotus was ever in Babylon is even a matter of doubt. But we do know for certain that the walls of Babylon were impressive. Those walls were built by slaves, some of whom were brought from Africa to work in the burning sun until they fell down dead. Interestingly enough, a significant part of the work was carried out by Babylonian citizens who had lost their freedom.

The Babylonians were eager borrowers. The credit trade was in the hands of a few rich families who charged high interest rates. Coins had not yet been invented, so the Babylonians traded in wheat and barley or gold and silver. The interest was substantial: 20 percent on loans of gold and silver, even 33 percent on crops. Each loan required collateral. Usually this was a house or a piece of land, as it is today. But in Babylon there was another option: yourself. Babylonians could offer themselves to their moneylenders as collateral. If they were not able to pay off their loans, the moneylenders would purchase them as slaves and they would end their days working on the impressive city walls.

It is hard to conceive of a more poignant example of the poison of indebtedness. Religions emphatically preach and warn against the incurring of debts, but all in vain. Today, three out of four households have debts consisting of consumer credit – excluding mortgages, that is, which are balanced by the value of the house. Credit card companies charge the "Babylonian" interest rate of 18 percent. Dreams evaporate because bills have to be paid.

Debts make the poor poorer and the rich richer. The billion-dollar debt of developing nations is a painful illustration. "Better to go to bed hungry than to wake up in debt," wrote Benjamin Franklin.

But even so.

Even so, that "pernicious debt" is also an extremely effective and powerful source of change and development. Nothing, in fact, makes a greater contribution to the progress of poor people in poor nations. Debt can also be a solution to poverty.

That's what this book is all about.

Jurriaan Kamp
Bentota, Sri Lanka

Elena and Juan

When she was 9 years old, Elena Huanca ran away from home after a dramatic family quarrel, fearful of her father. Somehow she managed to make her way from poverty-stricken Aymara, a village in rural Bolivia, to the capital city of La Paz. Wandering and homeless, she survived by earning money doing cleaning here and there. When she was almost 20, she decided to go into business. She set up a table on the street corner and offered passers-by a glass of warm *api* – a traditional drink made by combining purple and yellow maize with sugar, cinnamon and lemon – and a *buñuelo* – a kind of flatbread.

Juan was one of her regular customers. Every morning on his way to work at the paint factory he had breakfast at her stand. Their daily chat developed into something more, and Elena and Juan decided to get married. They organized their lives around Elena's *api* business. Juan helped her as much as he could before and after work. Contact with Centro de Fomento a Iniciativas Económicas (FIE) brought about a breakthrough in their existence. In 1998 Elena first borrowed $3,000 to purchase ingredients, an investment that resulted in considerable savings in transportation costs. In two years, after paying back the loan, Elena and Juan borrowed another $3,000. With this second loan they rented their own café nearly opposite her street stand, along with six tables and a television. Juan left his other job. Their turnover more than doubled from an average of 80 bolivianos (around $11) to about 200 bolivianos (almost $28) a day. Today about 70 customers visit the café each day, twice as many on weekends. A customer pays two and a half bolivianos (34 cents U.S.) for a glass of *api* with a *buñuelo*.

With their increased income, Elena and Juan's first priority is to provide support for their 21-year-old son, who is starting a videogame business. But they have other plans as well. Elena has her eye on the shop next to the café, which would double their floor space. And they're getting cable television – cost, $35 a month – so their customers will be able to watch CNN en Español. Elena is convinced that this extra service will attract more customers, so she'll be able to hire a couple of waitresses too.

FIE is ready to continue backing Elena and Juan with new loans. What's their dream? Elena, 42, beams. "A house of our own..." And then, with modest hesitation, "...and a car. I'm still young."

A Failure of Good Intentions
and a Promising Alternative

In the summer of 2002, a new government took office in the Netherlands without a ministry of development co-operation. After more than 30 years, the government eliminated the post that had been proof of the importance attached by the Netherlands to a more equitable relationship between a rich North and the poor South. Indeed, the Netherlands (along with the Scandinavian countries) is one of the few countries that comply with the standard set by the United Nations stipulating that a minimum of 0.6 percent of the national income be spent on development co-operation. The first Dutch minister of development co-operation, T.H. Bot, took office in 1965. Jan Pronk, a member of the Den Uyl cabinet of 1973, was almost the international personification of Western development policy.

Has this splendid example finally played itself out? Are fighting poverty and striving for international solidarity no longer priorities for the Dutch government? Not by a long shot. Even without a minister, the Netherlands will easily satisfy the 0.6 percent development standard. Yet hiding behind this remarkable step taken by the Dutch government is an inescapable fact. After 30 years of development aid or development co-operation, there is but one conclusion to be drawn: It's not working this way. The gulf between poor and rich in the world is only getting bigger.

Development aid was initiated 30 years ago in the tradition of the Marshall Plan, which had helped put Europe back on its feet after the Second World War. The idea was that large-scale investments in infrastructure and industry – in harbours, power stations, roads, dams and communication – would stimulate economic growth, pave the way toward eliminating hunger and poverty, and promote progress in poor countries. The hard reality is that despite the billions of dollars spent in assistance, the post-war European success has not been repeated in developing countries. Each year, $60 billion is still going from rich countries to poor countries. Despite this, 80 percent of Kenyans are still without electricity. Bangladesh was given more than $30 billion in assistance over a 30-year period, but the country is poorer now than it was before all that money arrived; Bangladesh is sardonically called "the Fifth World." These are not exceptions. The same is true of Bolivia and Uganda, indeed of the bulk of Africa, Asia and South America. The British economist Susan George addressed the problem in her book *A Fate Worse than Debt*: "Never before have so few been so wrong with such devastating consequences for so many."

Naturally, the numerous civil wars that came on the heels of independence in many developing countries had their destructive results on economic development. Naturally, there are sporadic examples of success. And naturally, there are statistics showing that the national per-capita income in poor countries is rising. But that last figure is an average pulled upwards by a small and increasingly rich elite; the poor masses are increasing and becoming even poorer. Gert van Maanen, former managing director of the development organization Oikocredit, says in *Internationale Samenwerking* (May 2002), "Much economic assistance gets no further than the richest 10 percent of the population."

The gulf between poor and rich is threatening the future. "There can be no talk of sustainable development without abolishing the gulf between poor and rich," says Marilou van Golstein Brouwers, senior fund manager at the Triodos Bank in the Netherlands. The differences are only getting bigger. Eighty-five percent of the money earned in the world ends up in the hands of the richest 20 percent of the population. The poorest 60 percent earn six percent. The billions spent on development each year don't bridge the ever-widening gulf, partly because the lion's share of the aid is "restricted." That is, the poor country is "permitted" to spend its donation on goods and services that must be purchased in the donor country. There are magnificent Mercedes buses at the airport in Colombo, Sri Lanka, but that "aid" doesn't provide work for a single Sri Lankan, nor does it contribute to a better future for Sri Lanka. All it does is provide the tourist with transportation in a pleasant, cool bus.

In the old, impoverished downtown area of Hyderabad in central India, I saw Muslim women stare through narrow slits in their black veils to watch an American television series full of glitter, gleaming limousines, excess and wealth. The message of luxury creates expectations, expectations that Hyderabad will never live up to in these women's lifetimes. This doesn't mean they and their brothers will turn to extremism in massive numbers, but it does mean that the chance of a few choosing the violent route – out of frustration and disappointment – is growing larger each day. Throughout history, economic deficit has almost always been a cause of war and violence. And modern war is called terrorism.

"Peace is not something that happens by accident. It is the product of civil equality." This statement appeared in the 2001 annual report of the Bolivian financial institution FIE. Ever since the attacks in the United States on September 11, 2001, the absence of equality is increasingly recognized as a source of international instability and a potential liability for the multinational business community. And that is why since 9/11, paradoxically enough, poverty has been more prominent than ever on the international political agenda.

For decades, the relationship between poor and rich was mainly the preoccupation of a group of progressive insiders: Jan Pronk, Novib, Oxfam, etc. Now it's a subject for government leaders and meetings of the G8, the group of the seven richest industrialized countries plus Russia. Recently, after years of standing by and watching economic conditions in Africa deteriorate, the G8 declared itself in favour of a major investment plan (Nepad) for that continent. *Newsweek* called it "Mbeki's New Deal." That description shows that the West is once again opting for a Keynesian approach to progress, with the predictable negative results. "Great plan, but for nine out of 10 Africans it won't mean a thing," was the severe judgment of Kimanthi Mutua, director of Kenya's K-Rep Bank.

"Development aid is the cause of our poverty. It's turned most of the people of Bolivia into beggars. Everyone is helping us. No one does anything himself anymore. We're in worse shape than we were 30 years ago," says Fernando Prado, director of Development Alternatives Inc. (DAI) in La Paz. Bolivian farms don't produce any more wheat today, for example, because during the 1980s the United States – with the best of intentions – gave its wheat surplus to Bolivia free of charge. The farmers couldn't match the offer of free wheat, so they started planting other crops. Ironically, in their desperation many chose the coca plant. Americans thus created a problem they are now doing everything in their power to combat.

When riding in a taxi in Delhi, the capital of India, we put our youngest daughter between us because she couldn't bear the sight of all the beggars at the traffic lights. Every time we stop there's an assault, with efforts to show us the most gruesome abnormalities and mutilations to evoke our sympathy. Begging is business, but it's a business of dependence, a business without prospects. In this relationship, charity – giving money away – is no solution, not even in the short term. It only makes the begging worse, and the beggar loses his dignity, his self-respect, and his future.

The most devastating effect of development aid is that poor people lose the skills they need to help themselves. After colonialism and the missionaries, the white jeeps of the non-governmental organizations ended up having the same influence. Over the years this fact has been recognized, of course, by successive ministers, their officials and development organizations. But, driven by the UN norm and the mantra "more is better," virtually no one has succeeded in embarking on a really innovative, effective course.

One more quote from the annual report of FIE: "We must design financial systems that work for the majority." Almost all aid is aimed at the formal economy of developing countries – there where the books are kept with a certain amount of care so the donor money is "wisely" spent. But three-quarters of the people only come in contact with the "informal economy," the only real economy for millions of the poor. It is an economy that isn't included in the statistics, and "officially" creates no jobs. In most poor countries, half the economic activity – and sometimes much more – takes place in the informal sector, an economy without accountants, rules or licenses, an economy consisting of people who for the most part cannot read or write. It is a *market* economy in the most literal sense of the word.

But whereas the official economic statistics of the developing countries show stagnation, the economy of the poor is going great guns. Creativity and inventiveness know no bounds. Delhi is a filthy city, but you won't find any garbage there. Every plastic bag, every piece of paper and every aluminium tin finds its destination. There's always someone collecting something because he knows that what he's collecting is of value to someone else. In the centre of La Paz, the capital of Bolivia, women walk around with mobile telephones chained to their bodies – the modern version of the telephone booth. You stop one of the women and make your call while she calculates the length of the call with a stopwatch. You pay by the minute. Simple, yes – but who comes up with such ideas? Not the local employees of the telephone company. No, this is a discovery made by poor people who want to earn money to survive.

Every day, millions of people make all sorts of products, engage in trade and perform services. They make pots and pans from scrap and furniture from discarded wood. They weave fabrics and sew clothing with machines that often run on illegally tapped electricity. They cultivate grain, vegetables and fruit and sell their harvest along the roadside. They work with metal and stone. All these activities take place in microbusinesses involving a husband, wife and children, and sometimes extra manpower. These businesses – and not the large-scale projects financed with foreign money – provide work and incomes for millions of poor people in developing countries.

These microbusinesses have the strength and capacity to grow, but poor people have no money for investments. Banks are not interested in them. The poor have no collateral for loans, let alone a proper address. They can go to the loan shark in the market, who lends money at five percent a day – sometimes more. Many small businesspeople choose this option because, despite the absurd rent, they see the opportunity to give their businesses a boost and thereby to prop up their families' ways of life. Others stagnate in their poverty because they don't have the money to realize their plans.

Wherever there is successful development co-operation you'll almost always find small-scale and locally rooted projects, projects connected to that "informal" reality of the masses. These projects contribute to the development of small-scale enterprises. Such little businesses have shown themselves to be the most effective weapons in the fight against poverty. In this way, a few individuals or a few dozen, perhaps a few thousand – but certainly not millions – take a step forward and quite often succeed in leaving poverty behind. These are projects in which attention, knowledge and organization are more important than money.

Back to my daughter, so eager to help but horrified by the hordes of sick, disfigured beggars. What can we do? We might open the window of the taxi and ask one of the beggar women about her problems. We might work with her and devise a plan for healing her wounds and putting her life on a different track. Because she too is a person who can make a contribution and whom fate has relegated to a dead-end line of work. Why shouldn't she go stand in the market with a mobile telephone on a chain?

One of the main characters in this book, Udaia Kumar of the Indian financial institution SHARE (Society for Helping and Awakening Rural Poor through Education), walked up to such a beggar woman and started a conversation. Why are you begging? Why don't you do something that will earn you some real money? The woman, whose name was Suvarna, said she didn't think she had the skill to do anything like that. Kumar convinced her to take out a small loan of 1,000 rupees ($20 U.S.) from his company, which provides so-called microcredit. With that money Suvarna bought pencils and pens, which she then sold at the village market. Kumar still remembers her beaming face when she came running up to him and shouted from a distance, "I made a sale, I made a profit." The loan was paid off. New loans followed, with which Suvarna built up her own small company. Today Suvarna is no longer begging. She's a successful small businesswoman with her own little house and an electric fan that provides relief from the heat of the Indian countryside.

"Helping people help themselves" is the motto of microcredit. It may not be the complete answer to the problem of world poverty, but it is the only approach that has resulted in proliferating successes in many parts of Asia, Africa and South America.

One metaphor for development co-operation is catching fish. First the rich countries send fish to the poor. Then they send fishing poles so the poor themselves can fish for their own sustenance. Next, the poor borrow money to buy the fishing poles. Finally they pay off their loans. This small-scale development aid doesn't cost any money, but it is effective. And the beauty of it is that the capital for procuring the credit doesn't have to come from the West.

Joanna

The idea came from the village priest near the town of Masindi in northern Uganda. He discovered the knitting machine while he was on a trip to Kenya and thought it might be a useful tool for women's activities in his village. Joanna Barwogaza was immediately interested. She raised and sold cassava, which provided extra income for the family – in addition to the salary of her husband, the teacher at the village school. Through the cassava trade she had come into contact with the Ugandan microcredit institution SOMED. She used a loan of 100,000 shillings ($60 U.S.) to buy extra cassava, which she sold at schools. She was always on the go, but the cassava was not a reliable source of daily income. It did not bring in enough money to enable her to send her two children to a private school, for instance.

But Joanna saw possibilities in the knitting machine. She could use it to make the jumpers for the uniforms for the local schools. With a 500,000-shilling ($275 U.S.) SOMED loan and some savings, she bought a second-hand knitting machine for 700,000 shillings ($384 U.S.). Customers were quick in coming thanks to her contacts with the schools.

Joanna now makes an average of three jumpers a day with the machine. She sells these jumpers for 20,000 shillings ($11 U.S.). The yarn costs 8,000 shillings ($4.40 U.S.). And with her daily profit of 12,000 shillings ($6.50 U.S.) she could easily pay off the 500,000-shilling ($275 U.S.) loan and the interest in six months. She is now the full owner of the knitting machine.

The jumper-production scheme has been a great success. All the local schools have approached Joanna because she can make the jumpers at a lower price than those ordered from Kampala, the capital city. Joanna is considering a new loan for a sewing machine so the various knitted parts of the jumpers can more easily be put together. And if she finds someone who also wants to learn to use the knitting machine, she'll buy a second machine to increase production.

The knitting machine has brought about drastic changes in the lives of Joanna and her family in a year and a half. Her children are now enrolled in a private school. She's bought some land on which a new house is being built, which she plans to rent out as long as her family lives in the teachers' residence. Joanna's future gets brighter with every jumper. Filled with enthusiasm, she feeds the yarn into the machine. Outside the sun is burning. The thick walls of the residence keep her living room pleasantly cool. A refrigerator and a television reveal the family's progress. "There are lots of schools to go," she says.

CHAPTER I

The Benefits of Fighting Poverty

At least 1,000 people are seated in the dining room of a hotel in San Francisco. White tablecloths, immense chandeliers, starched waiters – everything breathes the air of grandeur. Applauding at their tables are the participants in the State of the World Forum, an annual congress at which the people of the established order get together to discuss innovative ideas. Standing on the dais is the speaker. He bows slightly, modestly, with his hands folded in front of his chest – the typical greeting of a Bengali or an Indian. The audience watches with glistening eyes; their applause goes on for several minutes. A room full of people who yearn for improvement and progress in the world have just listened to a story about an initiative that is actually eliminating poverty. This was no argument on behalf of an inspiring idea; this was a report about what's actually happening.

The speaker is Muhammad Yunus of Bangladesh, and the story he told – and keeps on telling – goes something like this:

Yunus was teaching economics at a university in the United States when Bangladesh broke away from Pakistan in 1971 after a bloody war. Yunus decided to go back and make his contribution to the reconstruction of his homeland. He became head of the economics faculty at Chittagong, the country's second-largest city with a harbour on the Gulf of Bengal. In 1974, while in Chittagong, he witnessed the second drama to hit Bangladesh within a short period of time: famine. "With my dissertation in my pocket I was teaching elegant economic theories about development," says Yunus. "Outside you could *see* people dying in the street. It was something I couldn't bear to watch. Everything I had learned seemed to mean nothing at all in the face of those dying people. I decided to concentrate on what *could* help them."

So Yunus adopted a new method. He replaced the popular bird's-eye-view approach with what he calls "worm vision": becoming so deeply engrossed in what's in front of you that you can touch it and smell it – and try to do something about it. In a village near the university, outside Chittagong, he saw a woman weaving bamboo stools. They were beautiful little stools, made with a great deal of skill. Yunus wanted to know how the woman was able to support herself. It turned out she earned about 50 paisa a day (two cents at the 1974 exchange rate). She was too poor to purchase the bamboo herself for weaving the stools so she borrowed the bamboo from the bamboo dealer who – in exchange – demanded she sell her stools only to him, for a price that he would set. It was a suffocating contract with no escape in sight for the poor woman. At the same time, the cost for purchasing bamboo was only five taka (22 cents at the time): 22 cents was enough to free this woman.

Yunus and one of his students decided to see if there were more people in need of similar amounts of money for their enterprises. After a few days they had found 42 people who needed 856 taka altogether ($27 u.s. at the time). "It was the biggest shock of my life," says Yunus. "I was deeply ashamed that I belonged to a society that was not able to provide 42 hard-working people with $27."

Yunus decided to issue 42 loans from his own pocket. The astonished people were given the money they needed, and were told that they could pay it back as soon as they were able to do so. In the meantime Yunus went to the local branch of a bank and proposed to the manager that loans be granted to the poor people he had met in the village. The manager nearly fell off his chair. "You're insane. That's impossible. How can you loan money to poor people? They don't have any collateral. They're not creditworthy."

Yunus went to the managing director of the local bank, where he met with the same combination of unwillingness and disbelief. The same thing happened with other high officials at other banks. Finally he found one bank that was prepared to issue loans, on the condition that Yunus himself guarantee them – but only after the bank had warned him several times that he was going to lose his money. The surprise came when the people who were given the loans paid back *every single* taka. Yunus returned to the bank full of enthusiasm. "You see, it's not a problem," he said. But the bankers were skeptical. "They'll think you're crazy if you loan them more money," they warned. "They'll never pay you back." Yunus did loan more money, however – and the poor entrepreneurs paid that back, too.

Then the bankers said it would only work in that one village. So Yunus went to another village. It worked there as well. Maybe so, said the bankers, but in five villages it won't work. It did, though. It also worked in 10. And in 20, 50 and 100. But the bankers continued to refuse to issue credit to the poor independently – without Yunus as guarantor. Yunus saw that it made no sense expending any more energy trying to convince the unwilling bankers. Then one morning it hit him: He'd start his own bank. A grameen bank (village bank). That was in 1976. More than 30 years later, the bank is the property of his 2.4 million poor borrowers – 95 percent of whom are women – and it's making a profit. In that 30 years, the Grameen Bank has issued more than $3.5 billion u.s. in minuscule microcredit – loans averaging $150 u.s. And so far, the poorest people in the world have paid back $3.2 billion, excluding interest. The average family size of each borrower is five, which means the Grameen Bank serves a total of about 12 million people, one-tenth the population of Bangladesh. This is accomplished with 12,000 employees working in 36,000 villages throughout the country.

Bengalis are given loans for seeds, enabling them to make even greater profits from their harvests because they're freed from the choking ties to the seed dealers and moneylenders who charge absurdly high interest rates. They're given loans to purchase animals, such as cows that supply them with milk – and thus with extra income. Borrowers who used to eat once or twice a day now enjoy three daily meals. They have more than one change of clothes. And some have used their loans to build houses with corrugated roofs and brick walls – palaces that had once been beyond their wildest dreams.

SMALL CHANGE

The Grameen Bank was the beginning of a worldwide microcredit revolution. From the Philippines to Sri Lanka, from Malawi to Uganda and from Bolivia to Honduras, microcredit has spread to more than 60 countries in every corner of the world. To Yunus' pride, microcredit even proved an effective means of promoting progress in depressed areas of American cities: the first transfer of "technology" from the developing world.

According to the Microcredit Summit Campaign – an international organization also started by Yunus – there are now 1,567 institutions worldwide active in issuing microcredit to 30 million families – or 150 million people – in 60 countries. The goal is to have reached 100 million of the poorest families in the world – 500 million people, a third of the world's population that lives in extreme poverty – by 2005.

Muhammad Yunus believes that credit is a human right that belongs in the United Nations' Universal Declaration of Human Rights.

Those 1,500-some institutions may exhibit enormous variety – which has to do with different conditions, different points of emphasis and different choices – but the similarities are even more striking. The most unusual thing about microcredit lending are the qualifying criteria. Whereas in an ordinary bank you normally qualify for a loan if you have a *minimum* amount of income or capital, microcredit institutions work the other way around: The entrepreneur must have a *maximum* income. In other words: He or she must be poor.

Candidates are selected by the employees of the institution. This is where a second obvious difference lies between microcredit and "ordinary" lending. Whereas banks expect their clients to come to them, the employees of microcredit institutions go out to visit their clients – on foot, by bicycle or by bus – to become acquainted with them within the environments of their own small businesses. That investment results in significantly higher personnel costs for the institutions, which explains why they charge such high interest rates that generally exceed market interest by at least 10 percent.

The speed at which loans are issued is also clearly different. Loan applications are often granted, and the money paid out, within a week. This quick procedure is possible because microcredit is not based on laws, rules and collateral, but on trust between the institution and the borrower. This basic principle renders complicated bureaucratic procedures superfluous. Issuing a microcredit loan does not require processing multiple copies of declarations, passports and other official documents (which isn't possible anyway, since such documents don't exist in the world of poor entrepreneurs). The agreement is laid down on one simple sheet of paper.

Loans usually amount to no less than $50; $5,000 is a rare maximum. In most microcredit institutions, the average loan is between $500 and $1,000. The loans are always short-term. Most loans are paid off within a year, usually in weekly payments. Loans that run longer than a year are extremely unusual.

The most striking difference between microcredit and "ordinary" lending has to do with the repayment percentages. Commercial banks in developing countries are accustomed to having to write off half their loans as irrecoverable. Microcredit institutions, on the other hand, report a 95 percent repayment percentage worldwide. That figure is the best proof of the creditworthiness of poor entrepreneurs in developing nations.

A microcredit revolution is taking place through people who, one way or another, were inspired by the story of the Grameen Bank. Grameen keeps popping up over and over again in the life stories of entrepreneurs and development workers – such as that of Benjamin Byarugaba in Uganda. As a public official, Byarugaba noticed a sizable gap between the government's development plans – which usually targeted the cities – and poverty in the countryside. So in 1990 he and a few friends and colleagues started a volunteer programme for rural development. They discovered the importance of lending as a means of stimulating small-scale activity in remote villages.

The initiative didn't get off the ground, however, until Byarugaba read an article on the Grameen Bank and decided to sign up for an international training programme given by the bank in Bangladesh. After four weeks he came home, full of enthusiasm, with a promise of support from the Grameen Trust if he were to start his own "Grameen" in Uganda. That he did. In 1998, with support from the Dutch Fred Foundation – via the Grameen Trust – SOMED was set up. SOMED then received support from Hivos as well.

SOMED has now made contact with 5,000 credit customers in the thinly populated countryside around Masindi in Uganda. To reach more people, SOMED needs more money, because although the borrowers are conscientious about paying off their loans, most of them want to take out new – and bigger – loans. Extra money must come from donors. And herein lies the threat to microcredit's continued success. Ever since the Grameen Bank proved that microcredit works, many donor countries and non-profit organizations have thrown themselves into copying that success. Frustrated by the failure of many other development strategies, they were grateful for the example of an effective alternative. But for the microcredit institutions, the relationship with donors means interference and dependence.

Benjamin Byarugaba is three hours late for our appointment in Kampala, held up by a conversation with a potential SOMED donor that ran overtime. It was an important conversation because Byarugaba and SOMED are determined to grow, issue more loans to more people, and do their utmost to fight poverty. In the end, the donor asked SOMED to develop a special credit product for farmers. Evidently agrarian support is part of the donor's policy. There's nothing wrong with that in and of itself, because poor, marginal farmers can profit from loans as well. The danger lies in the conference rooms of the donor's office. If in the future someone were to opt for a new policy – a minister, say, or a director – it could bring an end to support for agrarian credit that SOMED has developed especially for this donor. Such policy breaks dominate the history of development aid.

This was the frustration of Kimanthi Mutua in Nairobi, Kenya. His mother was concerned about the fate of the Kenyan poor. Under her guidance they produced things that she in turn sold to Third World shops in Europe. Thus fighting poverty had played a part in Mutua's childhood, and it was taken for granted that after he got his diploma in accountancy he would devote his talents to the poor of Kenya. In 1984 he set up an organization for rural development, the Kenya Rural Enterprise Program, or K-Rep. K-Rep was a pioneer in issuing microcredit loans in Kenya. Mutua spent years going from donor to donor with K-Rep, but finally he became so angry about the changes the donors imposed on him that he began searching for an alternative. He found it in Bolivia: a microcredit institution that functions like a regular bank – a bank that has permission from the central bank to manage savings, and that uses those savings to finance loans for its customers. It was an independent, self-supporting institution.

A statutory change was required to make this possible in Kenya, but since 1999 the K-Rep Bank, the first microfinancing bank in Kenya, has been a fact. The bank was set up with help from foreign capital, provided in part by the Triodos Bank in the Netherlands. The office of the K-Rep Bank is distinguished-looking and modern. It is in no way inferior to the offices of other "ordinary" banks. Only the building's location departs significantly from the norm. Whereas all the other banks have their offices in the tall buildings of downtown Nairobi, the K-Rep Bank is housed in a slum at the edge of the city – one of the areas where the bank is active. Mutua looks out from his director's office over a typical vista of rickety shacks made from scavenged material.

The transformation into a bank has given K-Rep an enormous shot in the arm. In the 10 years preceding its founding in 1990, K-Rep collected 300 million shillings ($4.1 million) from donors used for providing microcredit. Since 1999, the K-Rep Bank has collected 500 million shillings ($6 million U.S.) from 13,000 savings customers. The bank never has to wait for a donor's decision before it can issue new loans.

But independence from the donor is not the only benefit. Providing a savings facility meets a great need among the poor. Marilou van

Golstein Brouwers, who is involved with 30 microfinancing institutions on behalf of the Triodos Bank, says, "Savings is often called 'the forgotten half' of microfinancing. The poor have always saved for emergencies and investments, but owing to the absence of banks with teller windows and savings accounts, they put their saving in cattle, land, jewellery or gold, or they hid their money in an old sock."

This kind of saving is plagued with disadvantages. Cattle are not liquid: You can't exactly cut off a goat's leg to pay for school fees. In addition, cattle require care, whereas money in the bank grows "automatically." When there's money in your shack it's hard to get a good night's sleep, and the same is true for the old sock. An extra disadvantage to hording cash is that there's always a family member or friend who needs money. In the tight social structure of the poor, wherein people depend on each other, it's difficult to resist such an appeal, and as a result the sock often turns out to be empty when you need money yourself. Investing your savings in land is also attractive to the poor. Land can be used as a field, which can be harvested to produce extra income. But land isn't always able to provide income at the moment you need it either.

Some countries have far-flung networks of postal banks or national banks that do reach the poor in the countryside. But then the nasty situation arises in which savings from the poor are used to finance big business. After all, big businesses are "creditworthy" and the poor are not, despite the fact that many banks in developing countries wrestle with losses in their credit portfolios of up to 50 percent. Yunus speaks of "charity institutions for the rich." The savings of the poor is not invested in the same region from which it was taken; the development of the countryside is neglected because money from the poor in rural areas flows to the rich in the cities.

Studies show that the need to save among the poor is even greater than their need for credit. When K-Rep became a bank in 1999, the institution had 9,000 borrowers. Now there are 16,000. But during the same period the number of savers rose from zero to 30,000. At the K-Rep Bank you can open a savings account with as little as a 1,000 shillings ($12.50 U.S.), and subsequent deposits of 100 shillings ($1.25 u.s.) are also possible. No other bank in Kenya offers that level of savings, and it meets the needs of the poor. The great need for savings facilities among the poor is also reflected in the example of the Indonesian state bank, the Bank Rakyat Indonesia (BRI). Since 1970 this bank has set up 3,600 branches in the Indonesian countryside to contribute to rural development. In 1983 the amount of savings deposited by the rural poor at BRI totalled only $18 million u.s. This was too small to meet the demand for credit in the countryside, and BRI suffered severe losses.

In 1983, BRI embarked on a new policy that included the introduction of group savings, which proved an interesting option for agricultural co-operatives. Withdrawal limits were also lifted from savings accounts. Before that time, a saver could only withdraw money twice a month. In eight years, the deposited savings grew from $18 million to $1.3 billion in 1991. Now BRI has over $2 billion in savings at its disposal, representing about 16 million savers (averaging $125 per savings account), while the credit portfolio contains $850 million and 2.5 million borrowers. The savings not only go a long way toward meeting the need for loans in rural India, but constitute an interesting source of profit for the bank. And the poor receive interest and unlimited access to their money.

The prospects for saving in developing countries are enormous. Loans only reach the people who have small businesses, whereas everyone is interested in saving. But realizing all those possibilities is no small task. Reserve banks impose strict regulations on banks. And that is understandable: After all, banks manage other people's money. Precautions must always be taken so that banks don't go bankrupt and savers don't lose their money. That's why a non-profit organization or other institution is allowed to issue microcredit (a reserve bank doesn't care whether the loans are paid off or not, since the borrowed money comes from donors), but is not allowed to manage the money of private savers.

In order to satisfy the requirements laid down by central banks, microfinancing institutions must really become banks themselves, as the Kenyan K-Rep has done. Several countries now have separate – and less demanding – legal regulations for microfinancing institutions, adapted to the special character of these institutions, which make it possible to manage deposited savings. Similar regulations are being developed in other countries. The transformation still requires a great deal from the microfinancing institutions. Mutua of κ-Rep Bank points out that a "savings office" needs many more facilities – such as safes and security – than a branch that only issues loans. κ-Rep has only three branches that manage the money of 30,000 savers in the Kenyan capital (κ-Rep serves its 16,000 credit customers with 25 branch offices). The countryside is still unexplored territory. A savings office has to be close to the people. Mutua says, "People are willing to make a single 100-kilometre trip to be provided with a loan, but with savings it's different. That's got to be available within half an hour." In the countryside that means having many small offices following the Indian model, and that demands a great deal of investment and a lot of time. But the Indonesian model also demonstrates that such offices are worth the trouble.

Mutua insists that the savings deposited by the poor should ultimately be the main source of financing for microfinancing institutions. The κ-Rep Bank now covers half its demand for credit with savings. In five years that will have to be 100 percent. On its way to that goal, the κ-Rep Bank now takes out commercial loans from other banks to fully meet its demand for credit. But the advantage of financing with savings is obvious. A saver receives six percent on his balance, while a commercial loan can easily require a payment of 12 percent interest. As a microfinancing institution expands its activities to the remote corners of a country, that difference in interest becomes increasingly important for the viability and financing of the business. This is because the cost of issuing loans and managing savings is higher in the countryside due to a poor infrastructure and lower population concentrations.

The commercial approach to microfinancing – independent of donors – is spreading rapidly. FIE in Bolivia, and BASIX and SHARE in India, are microfinancing institutions that, like the Kenyan κ-Rep, cover the financing of demands for credit with capital that comes partly from abroad and is partly made up on commercial loans. SOMED in Uganda has not gone so far, but "within five years" it wants to become "an independent financial institution that can function without the support of donors." Reaching that goal requires microfinancing institutions to be profitable. Companies that lose money cannot easily attract shareholders, and the commercial sector will not issue loans to such businesses.

According to the mission statement of BASIX in India, "BASIX strives for a competitive return to enable it to attract commercial capital on a continuous basis." That "competitive return" consists mostly of a percentage comparable with the interest on government bonds; the microfinancing sector does not sacrifice its primary goal of fighting poverty to pursue a level of profit competitive with the returns made on the stock exchange. This is not a point of view that attracts every shareholder, but for the time being there are enough market parties – such as the Triodos Bank in the Netherlands – that are prepared to settle for a somewhat lower return if it means contributing to combatting poverty in developing countries. Pilar Ramirez of FIE says, "We want to preserve our social mission. That is why we have been careful in selecting our shareholders. They must be prepared to accept a lower return. Fighting poverty in an effective way should also be regarded as profit."

It seems paradoxical: profit-oriented institutions that fight poverty. Mutua of the Kenyan K-Rep Bank sees no contradiction: "It's a creative tension that is necessary for innovation." Others claim that the pursuit of profit keeps the microfinancing institutions from searching out the poorest of the poor. It is always tempting to issue more credit to successful, less poor entrepreneurs – with which more can be earned – than relatively expensive, small loans to as many very poor entrepreneurs as possible.

But a study carried out in 2000 by David Gibbons and Jennifer Meehan of the Malaysian network for financial services to the truly poor, CASHPOR, shows that the campaign against poverty being fought by microfinancing institutions is not negatively influenced by profit-making ambitions. As a matter of fact, it is thanks to this profit that the institutions have the money they need to offer microcredit loans to an increasing number of poor people, and that they are more effective than the donor-financed initiatives with which microcredit got started in many places. "The only way to reach really large numbers is with a profit-oriented strategy and financial independence," write Gibbons and Meehan. Ultimately, a wide range of microcredit will always be beneficial to the poorest of the poor – in the form of employment, for instance – even though it sometimes comes indirectly by way of loans to less poor entrepreneurs. The scale of microcredit lending seems to be more important for fighting poverty than an exclusive focus on the poorest of the poor.

So for microfinancing institutions, profit is a crucial condition for success. Say you want to issue microcredit averaging $150 to 500,000 people, which means you need $75 million. If you want to reach the 100 million poorest families – the goal of the Microcredit Summit Campaign – you need 100,000,000 x $150 = $15 billion. Where is that money going to come from, if the total annual development aid worldwide amounts to $60 billion? There's just not enough donor money to fight poverty in this way.

Once again, the example of Bank Rakyat Indonesia is illustrative. The bank now provides a total of $850 million in loans to microenterprises in Indonesia. It is inconceivable that the Indonesian government would make such a sum available for the development of the microsector. The material profit for the shareholder is a condition for the social profit of fighting poverty.

The commercial approach is clearly leading the way in the microfinancing sector. Following in the footsteps of Muhammad Yunus and the Grameen Bank, microcredit was first taken up by non-governmental organizations motivated by charity. Small groups were reached with small programmes. Now that microcredit has proven itself and is ready to reach millions, the next step calls for professionalism. Charity and independence make way for mutual respect and customer service. Being self-supporting and independent have become attainable goals because the poor also have proven to be savers. The $27 that Muhammad Yunus gave to 42 poor Bengalis was the beginning of microcredit. Thirty years later, microcredit has evolved into microfinancing – supported by the savings of the poor themselves, without being dependent on development aid. That is the profit of fighting poverty.

Deshaboina

He heard an extraordinary bit of news in a neighbouring village: An organization had arrived that issued loans that could be used for making investments. So Deshaboina Ramulu, from the village of Ilapuram, was the first to knock on the door of the new branch of the Indian microcredit institution BASIX in the nearby district centre of Suryapet in the state of Andhra Pradesh. Deshaboina had long been saving to buy a second milk buffalo to generate extra income. But a buffalo cost 7,000 rupees ($150 U.S.) at the time, and he had only saved 4,000 rupees ($80 U.S.). With a loan from BASIX of 10,000 rupees ($200 U.S.) he could even buy two buffalo. He would have one year to pay off the loan, plus 24 percent interest. The extra weekly expense of about 240 rupees ($5 U.S.) was no problem because the proceeds from the milk of the three buffalo, which he brought to Suryapet himself every day by bike, amounted to more than 700 rupees ($15 U.S.) a week. On top of that, Deshaboina could save up to invest in his three-acre field. There he planted peanuts, sorghum and millet, not only for his family (himself, his wife and three children), but also for selling at market.

With his new savings, the farmer had a well dug for the irrigation of his field, but the attempt failed. To make matters worse, one of the buffalo died. Insurance to cover such catastrophes is not yet available in rural India. Yet Deshaboina succeeded in paying off his loan. With a second loan of 15,000 rupees ($325 U.S.) he bought two more milk buffalo – and then another two with a third BASIX loan. Now, after the birth of two calves, he owns a total of nine buffalo. He also had part of his land levelled so he could cultivate rice, which brings in even more, both at the market and in terms of status. A family that eats rice instead of sorghum enjoys a certain prestige.

We talk under the lean-to in front of his simple one-room stone house. An electric clock and a television set are proudly displayed to passersby. The surrounding lot is covered with sand and dust and merges into an unpaved road. Playing children create clouds of dust. Deshaboina cannot read or write. His two daughters and his son are now no longer attending the public school across the road, but – for 6,000 rupees ($125 U.S.) a year – go to a private school in Suryapet. His wife no longer works as a hired agricultural labourer but takes care of the buffalo and works around the house. This too is an important step forward. Deshaboina is determined to use his new savings to risk another attempt at digging a well on his field. If he can cultivate rice alone, his family's life will be even better.

CHAPTER 2

Collateral or Trust?

The Kenyan economy has been in a recession for 25 years. Whatever the promise of Africa may have been has become bogged down in a typical mishmash of politics and corruption that nips every advancement in the bud. Kenya is pining for new political leadership, new courage. "Nothing is impossible for a willing heart" it says in decorative letters on the window of the taxi, once imported from London. That's all there is to hold onto.

Downtown Nairobi is still reminiscent of the prospects of the past. Tall buildings with well-known international logos line the broad boulevards. Gigantic billboards are evidence that the stagnation is not total. Spacious green parks offer rest and refreshment. Lining the avenues are the colonial villas, so recognizable throughout the former British empire. Nairobi is not Africa. The taxi moves down wide boulevards past whitewashed walls and iron fences. Wealth and crime are bound together in a vicious escalating circle. The walls are higher, the fences more threatening, the crime increasing.

The farther we go from the centre the closer we get to Africa. The little markets are fuller, the buildings simpler. This simplicity turns almost imperceptibly into slums. You are in Kawangware. Here and there you still see a few concrete buildings of two or three stories. Around them extends an endless plain of shabby improvisation. Suddenly the long Naivasha Road changes from a level asphalt avenue leading to a suburb to a collection of deep, sandy pits where cars, trucks, buses and scooters advance inch by inch, simmering and smoking.

So we're late for our appointment with Pattrick, the staff member from k-Rep, who is waiting for us at the agreed spot. No problem. Nothing is ever a problem, which is not to say that everything is possible or feasible. Following Pattrick, we push our way through the busy market. A heavy downpour that morning has created an extra impediment. Following a narrow alley to the left, then to the right, we end up in a small open area bounded by three open huts. Sitting in one of the huts are 30 women and two men on white plastic garden chairs. Most of the women are dressed in wide flowered dresses, their heads wrapped in colourful scarves. The women lead the discussion. The two men are silent. Our greeting is met with a friendly response, but the activities continue without interruption. All around us, dirty, crumpled shilling notes are passed from hand to hand. Here and there someone writes something in large letters, and on every lap there's a small notebook. We're witnessing the weekly gathering of a lending group. This group, which consists of people who have been issued loans by the κ-Rep Bank, gets together every Wednesday morning at 10 o'clock to pay their interest and principal to one of the bank's staff members.

Pattrick's meeting consists of six groups of five borrowers. The groups of five come together in groups to simplify the repayment of the loans to the bank staff member. Pattrick is responsible for 15 such groups, totalling more than 400 borrowers. To those 400 people he issues a total of about 15 million shillings in credit annually, which comes to about $450 per person. These loans are paid off in an average of 26 weeks, or half a year. The maximum time limit for a loan is one year.

The word "credit" comes from the Latin verb *credere* – to believe. And that is exactly what banks do not do. They do not trust their borrowers to pay back the borrowed money. That is why they require collateral. You may borrow money as long as you offer something by which the bank – in the event of emergency – can recover its money. But poor people have no possessions that they can use as collateral. It took the patriarch of microcredit, Muhammad Yunus, to think up a solution to that problem.

Yunus turned to the poor villagers of Bangladesh, to whom he wanted to issue loans, and decided to involve them in the problem. These discussions resulted in the decision to divide the borrowers into groups of five to 10 first to simplify loan repayment. Those groups would be composed by activity: rickshaw groups, bamboo-weaving groups, milk buffalo groups. Then it was decided that all transactions would take place out in the open in the village during weekly meetings. Each person had to be able to see who was being issued what kind of loan, and who was paying off what amount: the more eyes the better. This approach took advantage of the strict social control that exists in the villages, but also protected the illiterate villagers from the "secrecy" that made them shy away from official dealings. In addition, this social control would protect the Grameen Bank from problems in loan repayment.

In order to reinforce the effect of social control, Yunus added a few rules. Not all five members of a group were given a loan at the same time. First, two people were given a loan, and if they proved in the following weeks that they could meet their payments promptly, the next group members were given a loan. Supplemental loans were only issued when everyone had fully paid the debts. In this way the group members had a stake in each other's good behaviour. If a borrower failed to stick to the agreement he put the others at a disadvantage – and he did this out in the open in the village square. The rule not only stimulated negligent borrowers to pay their debts, but it also stimulated solidarity. If someone got into trouble because of sickness or some kind of setback, it was in the group's interest to help. Finally, it was decided that each group member was obliged to save at least one taka (four cents at the time) to build up an emergency fund.

The group rules took the place of collateral. The borrower who did not stick to the rules, did not come to the meetings, did not pay his debt, and did not save, harmed not only himself but the others as well. The Bengali villagers accepted that and made sure they paid off their loans.

The Grameen Bank's system of "social collateral" was adopted by most of the world's microcredit institutions and has now been further developed and perfected. For instance, borrowers were made expressly responsible for the loans of their fellow borrowers within the lending group. If one of the borrowers failed to pay his debt, the bank could claim the money from the other group members. But the basic principle – that of trust – remained central: trust between the bank and the borrower, but also trust among the five borrowers within each group. And because trust is important, personal relationships are taken seriously.

"The only due diligence that we do is a character assessment of the borrower," says Director Kimanthi Mutua of к-Rep. Ordinary banks require collateral because they do not know their clients. Microfinancing institutions, on the other hand, want to become acquainted with their customers. It's one of the terms of the relationship. A customer makes contact with an ordinary bank at the teller window. Staff members of microfinancing institutions don't stay at the office; they meet and visit their clients at the market. Such staff members can easily spend three-quarters of their day outside. They examine whatever machines, stocks and raw materials are on the premises of the potential borrower. They talk with his family members and his neighbours. And naturally they talk with the borrower himself. This practise builds familiarity and trust. We trust you and your project, the institution finally says, and while that message gives the entrepreneur a financial boost, it also gives him something that may be even more important: recognition.

Familiarity and trust also play a role in organizing the lending group. Borrowers are exceedingly cautious about choosing their group partners; after all, their financial future depends on them. John Muigai, a charcoal dealer from the Kenyan countryside, clearly remembers arriving in Nairobi more than 10 years ago. He wanted to take out a к-Rep loan to further develop his business, but he didn't know anyone. It took quite awhile before he was able to find people who were willing to start a lending group with him (also see Portrait IV): The absence of trust resulting from unfamiliarity initially got in the way of his credit. In addition, the microfinancing institutions generally do not allow family members to sit in the same lending group. Most groups are formed by fellow craftsmen or by people from different trades active in the same neighbourhood.

Social collateral is an almost-perfect system. Repayment rates for microfinancing institutions exceed 95 percent worldwide. And

Pattrick, the employee from the K-Rep Bank, says he doesn't even notice if a borrower misses one of her weekly payments. Her colleagues in the group take over the payment automatically and deal with the matter among themselves. None of the institutions ever has to restructure a loan.

The group system within the SHARE microfinancing institution in India serves yet another function. SHARE works with groups of five borrowers, all women. Each week, eight groups of five meet together with a SHARE employee. Any new loan must be approved at that meeting by the 40 women – along with the SHARE employee. This creates a certain market regulation. Otherwise, poor entrepreneurs have the tendency to choose the same activities. This would result in too little diversification, which would limit the prospect of economic development in general and the success of the individual entrepreneur in particular.

A woman whose neighbour is selling vegetables by the roadside decides to open a vegetable stand of her own without giving it much thought. But at the end of the day there are too many vegetable stands and too few customers. By requiring that every new loan be approved by 40 women, SHARE overcomes this problem. The women guide each other in more lucrative directions.

SHARE's approach is unique, if nothing else. Since 1992, SHARE hasn't lost a single rupee in repaid loans. That's a unique record, not only in the world of microfinancing but in the established financial world. Udaia Kumar, founder and director, conducts the institution like a military operation. His employees never leave their weekly meetings without a perfect result. That's called zero tolerance even in rural India. Experience has taught that the refusal of SHARE employees to leave meetings results in the full repayment of debts within a half an hour.

This hard approach also has a down side. A report on SHARE put out by *Microcredit Ratings International* in 2001 said the institution has a relatively high client turnover, which "is a direct consequence of the high level of discipline expected of borrowers." On the other hand, SHARE is owned by more than 26,000 borrowers, each of whom has invested capital to the tune of 500 to 1,000 rupees ($11 to $22 U.S.). That shareholding creates a strong connection between SHARE and its clients.

Kikingura is half an hour's ride by car over unpaved roads from Masindi in thinly populated northern Uganda. Growing along the roadside are tobacco, cassava and sugar cane – and plenty of banana trees. There isn't a fence or barrier to be seen, but each tree has an owner. A tree can produce one large bunch of bananas a year. Each bunch of about 100 bananas or more brings in 2,000 shillings on the market (less than $1.25 U.S.) – a fortune in the countryside, but you never hear about a bunch of bananas being stolen from an unguarded tree.

Early on a Friday morning, dozens of women are sitting under reed parasol-like roofs in the dusty market square. The whole surrounding village consists of mud and straw. Children run around barefoot. Here and there you see a bike. The motorcycle of an employee from SOMED creates an incongruous noise. On this particular morning, 72 SOMED borrowers are gathering in Kikingura. It is a special meeting. Not only are the weekly payments being processed in the presence of the SOMED employee, but a theme is being dealt with as well.

One of the women has been talking about "good customer relations" and this presentation has sparked a lively discussion. Everyone is talking about her own experiences with customers at the weekly Sunday market, when Kikingura is the region's commercial centre. Such sessions, which in the case of SOMED are organized by one of the borrowers, illustrate the fact that the concerns of the lending group reach further than social collateral and repayment. The group gatherings provide support for the borrowers in many other respects. The last thematic session of SOMED borrowers in Kikingura was about tension in the family, but the women have given each other advice about diarrhea and the danger of dehydration in children. Borrowers from the Grameen Bank endorse 16 decisions that extend far beyond their financial relations with the bank. They make promises among themselves to keep their families small, to allow their children to go to school, to drink water only if it comes from pumps or has been boiled, and not to accept or give dowries.

Despite the obvious success of the lending groups, some microfinancing institutions opt for another kind of policy. Pilar Ramirez, the founder and director of the Bolivian FIE, fiercely opposes the use of lending groups. "It's insulting to impose extra conditions on poor people. They already have to do so many things that other people don't have to do: They must walk to fetch water and wood for cooking, and they often have no access to electricity. This extra condition stigmatizes them; it treats them like children. It has the same effect as when children with a disability are put together in a special school. They're stuck there forever," says Ramirez. She wanted FIE to issue loans to the poor just as ordinary banks lend to the rich, with no difference. If the poor are as creditworthy as everyone else – and this was apparent from the Grameen Bank example, Ramirez's inspiration – then they should be given credit like everyone else. Individually.

Assisted by a friendly lawyer, Ramirez found a solution in the law. She learned that it was possible to issue a loan to someone if another person was willing to guarantee it. This happened to be an existing practise, but it always involved poor people taking out loans and rich people – the priest, for example – standing surety for them. Ramirez found that stigmatizing as well. The lawyer told her, however, that the guarantor could come from the same low-income group as the borrower. The point was that he had to be in a position to pay back the loan. Now, nine out of 10 loans issued by the FIE are signed by two people from the same social environment. Friends stand surety for friends, and colleagues for colleagues. "That was a completely new idea," Ramirez says in retrospect. For the entrepreneurs it meant having much easier access to credit than having to form a lending group.

Ramirez recalls one remaining obstacle. The lawyer had said family members could not stand surety for each other – just as lending groups could not consist of family members. "I thought that was ridiculous. Family is the only thing poor people have. So you do everything you can to keep from antagonizing your family. I always said that the best guarantor is your mother-in-law. We've proven that family members are the best guarantors."

Ramirez's contrary approach has not had the slightest negative effect on the microcredit success of FIE. Only about seven percent of FIE's credit portfolio is regarded as risky. That's quite remarkable since the repayment conduct is not determined by a weekly gathering of the lending group. "The weekly gathering is one of the myths of microfinancing," says Ramirez. Each FIE borrower is expected to take the initiative to visit the office each month and make a payment. And that's what happens – without social compulsion. Eighty percent of the borrowers make their payments within five days.

"We believe people will pay their debts. And apparently our clients pick up on that," says Ramirez. Most late payers ring up and explain that a problem has arisen which is keeping them from paying on time. FIE employees are given daily lists indicating which clients are in arrears. Sometimes the client is contacted by telephone if necessary. Telephone? "Yes," says Ramirez, "the mobile telephone is the one possession that everyone has now."

The Indian microfinancing institution BASIX also issues individual loans. BASIX found its own method for guaranteeing maximum repayment involving the relationship of trust between employees and clients. The salary of BASIX employees is linked to the repayment conduct of their clients. If the instalment amounts to more than 97 percent, the employee gets 1/8 of the posted interest on the loan. If the instalment amounts to more than 95 percent, the employee gets 1/10, etc. With this method, good employees in the field end up with higher salaries than their directors back in the office, *and* BASIX gets its loans paid back.

Director and founder Vijay Mahajan of BASIX says, "The only way to get good new contacts is to maintain good contacts with the clients you already have. In order to keep earning a good salary, you must invest in the relationship with your present clients and in recruiting new ones." So the employees at BASIX end up with a salary based on trust – entirely in the tradition of microfinancing.

John

His parents' divorce was the final blow for the fragile existence of John Muigai in rural Kenya. He barely managed to finish primary school, and there was no money to continue his education. As a boy of 12 he went to Nairobi, where he sold the charcoal that his mother brought in every week in a rented truck from their village, 200 kilometres from the Kenyan capital.

When the microfinancing institution κ-Rep started its operations in 1993, John signed up. At first it was not easy for him, a stranger in the big city, to find four fellow borrowers, but finally he succeeded. John invested his first loan of 10,000 shillings ($120 u.s.) in establishing a grocery next to his charcoal business. He used a second loan of 25,000 shillings ($300 u.s.) to expand his stock.

Then John noticed that customers kept asking if he knew about any available houses or shops. This gave him an idea. He would approach landlords and offer to find tenants for their properties. That was how John's real-estate business got started in the slums of Kawangware. He got a commission of 10 percent of the annual rent he was able to obtain for the landlords. It was an enormous success. John's monthly turnover skyrocketed, thanks to several loans from κ-Rep. His turnover in 1993, including his charcoal business, was 15,000 shillings. Almost 10 years later, the monthly turnover of Fortcom, his real-estate business, is 7 million shillings ($3,800 u.s.), and he has an office in one of the few serious commercial buildings in Kawangware. John now invests in the construction of such buildings. He supports his widely extended family and pays school fees for his nephews and nieces. His mother is enjoying a peaceful old age in her village in the countryside.

John looks back at his success. "Without κ-Rep I never could have made it. For people with an idea, access to credit is crucial. κ-

Rep made me what I am today." He realizes that his story is an exception. "Too many people start these kinds of small businesses. They decide to sell vegetables because their neighbour is doing it. But imitation is not the basis of success."

John still does his banking with the microfinancing institution. His present loans amount to 500,000 shillings ($275 u.s.). "Borrowing money from an ordinary bank takes forever," he says. "K-Rep knows me and I get my money within a week." Soon it's time for him to leave, but before driving away in his gleaming car he tells us through the open window, "You know, I still have contact with the friends from my charcoal-dealing days."

CHAPTER 3

Indian Jewels

After more than 10 years of intensive work combatting poverty in rural Uganda, Benjamin Byarugaba has come to an unavoidable conclusion: Women must lead the fight against poverty in the developing world. We're speaking at the headquarters of the Support Organization for Micro-Enterprises Development (SOMED), the microcredit institution Byarugaba founded in Masindi, Uganda.

Headquarters. That's a ponderous term for an organization with only three branches staffed by 14 people – but with 5,000 borrowers, too. The headquarters consists of four small rooms that all open into each other. There's just been a power failure, but SOMED's three computers run on the generator chugging away outside in the main street. And then there's the dust. Dust everywhere. Thirty kilometres south of Masindi, the asphalt road from the capital city of Kampala comes to an end. North of the town, a jungle begins that runs for about 40 kilometres and ends at the banks of the Nile.

"Women don't earn money. That's one of the main causes of poverty in the world. Since time out of mind, families have depended on men's income. Women never get out of the kitchen," says Byarugaba. It's more than a cultural phenomenon. It's more than a simple observation of the wave of emancipation that has yet to reach the rural areas of the developing world. It's more than the importance of equality. It's a matter of missed economic opportunities, not only for the women themselves but also for the whole family, for the children's future, for the future of the developing world.

It's not that women don't do anything. On the contrary, the lion's share of all the work undertaken in developing countries is probably done by women. But those efforts don't show up on the radar screen. Women often spend hours walking back and forth to a water pump. They gather wood so they can cook – and that requires hours of walking, too. If those "lost" hours could be put to more productive use, the household's earning capacity would increase enormously. That's what Benjamin Byarugaba thinks. That's why 80 percent of the SOMED loans are issued to women. Hanging on the wall over Byarugaba's desk is the SOMED mission statement: "Our goal is to improve the position of the most disadvantaged, economically active poor – especially women – by issuing them small loans, so the active poor can gain enough confidence to create the kind of prosperity that results in satisfying lives."

Attending to the needs of women is a worldwide feature of microfinancing. The microfinancing institution FIE in Bolivia began with the same focus. FIE is the initiative of five Bolivian women under the direction of the previously mentioned Pilar Ramirez. On the way to our first meeting I happen upon Ramirez standing at the teller's window on the ground floor of the FIE office in La Paz. Ramirez is withdrawing money. She starts laughing when she sees me. "Bank directors need money too," she says. "Although not too many people start their own bank so they can withdraw money themselves." We walk the four sets of stairs up to Ramirez's office on the top floor. Panting. The thin air of La Paz, located at an elevation of 4,000 metres (13,000 feet), is a formidable opponent. As we catch our breath I drink coca tea – not exactly delicious, but the Bolivians swear it helps deal with the altitude.

In the mid-1980s – after the restoration of democracy in Bolivia – Ramirez and four colleagues devoted themselves to the cause of the United Nations refugee organization (the United Nations High Commissioner for Refugees, UNHCR), which was supervising the return of refugees. The women saw that the UNHCR approach yielded little fruit. Returning refugees were given subsidies and gifts, and when the money was up they came back to the UNHCR for more.

That frustration put Ramirez on the track of the Self Employed Women's Association (SEWA) of India and the Grameen Bank, both of which had been successful with microcredit lending. Earlier in her life Ramirez had worked as a psychologist for Bolivian mining co-operatives. "I was supposed to focus my attention on family conflicts and mental illness. But what really interested me was the fact that the people in those communities worked so hard but hadn't a clue about how to handle money. They rarely made any profit. That's why I wanted to learn more about the economics of development. And because I was involved in the political women's movement, my question was more specific: How do you improve the position of women?"

In Ramirez's experience, women in Bolivia had hardly any access to employment. They lacked the knowledge necessary for running their own businesses, and they had no access to financing. Ramirez also knew the traditional approach of development aid and subsidies wouldn't change anything. "I saw that microcredit could solve all those problems."

Ramirez proposed converting the UNHCR gifts to the refugees into loans. But in 1985 such a suggestion – in the established "development world" – was doomed to fall on deaf ears. So Ramirez and four colleagues struck out on their own and founded FIE, making it Bolivia's first organization to issue microcredit. More such organizations quickly followed.

In the beginning, FIE's distinguishing feature was that it limited its loans to small microproduction businesses. In Ramirez's opinion, only individual production could make a substantial contribution to a country's economic development. She felt that when you trade in products you don't get very far in the end. Finally that policy was abandoned when Ramirez realized that such an exclusive focus on production discriminated against women. "The first economic activity that women get involved in is small-scale trading. They deal in clothing, for example. Then they discover they can earn more if they make the clothing themselves. So production is a logical second step," says Ramirez.

In 1998, FIE was converted from a non-governmental organization into an independent, profit-oriented microfinancing institution. Today FIE also finances a limited number of small-scale trading companies – mainly owned by women. Women make up more than half the FIE clientele. But recognizing the needs of women is no longer a goal in itself. "You couldn't talk about the position of women back then without including the economic dimension. That brought me to microcredit. But the goal is to make sure that microcredit works, that the borrower is better off economically. If on top of that you've got to decide whether a loan will help a woman as a woman in her environment, you make it unnecessarily complicated. We're not starting in with that."

But even if helping women is not a goal in itself, microcredit has made an enormous impact on the position of women. It's no coincidence that women are the main focus of microfinancing institutions. If you really want to combat hunger and poverty, you've got to go where the women are. That's what the bank discovered. Women experience hunger and poverty much more intensely than men. They cook – or they don't if there's nothing to eat. They eat,if their husbands and children have already eaten. And if women earn an income, they spend it on their families – more than men do. Women are closer to the children. That means that to focus on women is to focus on the future.

At the State of the World Forum in San Francisco, Muhammad Yunus movingly described how the first loan affected the life of a woman in Bangladesh: "She doesn't sleep the night before getting the loan. She lies tossing and turning, wondering whether she should take the loan at all. As a girl and as a woman she has caused so many problems for her family [the dowry is still a widespread custom in Bangladesh]. She doesn't want to do anything that will make her more of a burden by not being able to pay back the loan. In the morning her friends come by and encourage her to join them, because they've decided to go in on this together, and the group will fall apart if she withdraws. So she agrees, for that reason, and she takes out her first loan for the equivalent of about $12 U.S. A treasure! She can't believe that someone would trust her with such a fortune. She trembles, and tears run down her cheeks. She promises herself not to disappoint the person who has given her such an enormous sum, to work very hard to pay back every cent. And she does. She begins with very small weekly instalments. She's got to pay back the entire amount, plus interest, within a year. Her first instalment is a staggering experience. She can do it – even though she didn't believe she could at first. She celebrates the second instalment as a triumph. And after one year, she's become another person. She has found herself. Everyone said she was worthless, but today she's someone who can do something. She can take care of herself and her family."

Issuing microcredit to women not only contributes more directly to the goal of combatting poverty, but it also is apparently better for the "financial health" of microfinancing institutions. The Indian financial institution SHARE, in Hyderabad in the state of Andhra Pradesh lends money only to women, and it hasn't lost a single rupee in the credit it's provided. Founder and Director Udaia Kumar sees a clear relationship between "100 percent women" and "100 percent repayment": "Women are much more responsible than men. They are also more eager to learn and less cocksure. That's why the path to combatting poverty and to the financial independence offered by microfinancing institutions takes place via women."

In the experience of the founders of the K-Rep Bank in Kenya and SOMED in Uganda, which are oriented exclusively towards women, women are much more prepared than men to form the lending groups on which the granting of credit in these institutions is based.

The social solidarity of women also forms the basis of a promising Indian movement that is now the largest microcredit programme in the world: self-help groups. These are groups of 15 to 20 poor women who meet together, save together and use their common savings to provide each other with credit. It's a phenomenon that has existed at least 30 years in India. Such a group might consist of women who occasionally work on the land. The typical goal of such a group is for the participating women to save one day's wages per month – 25 to 30 rupees, or 55 to 65 cents U.S. In this way a woman can save about 300 rupees – $6.50 – a year.

It's a self-supporting system in which no microfinancing institutions or other external sources of financing are customarily involved. That autonomy has its drawbacks: The total amount of savings determines the total amount of extended loans. Research shows that the average loan a women's group can issue a member amounts to about 4,000 rupees ($87). The purchase of a milk buffalo – a popular step taken by rural women to generate more income – takes at least 8,000 rupees ($175). So by "helping yourself" you don't get very far.

The government of the state of Andhra Pradesh recognized this 10 years ago. Andhra Pradesh is one of the most deprived states in India, where almost half the population lives under the official poverty line. The government decided to give the groups a boost. First they donated a sizable amount to these women's groups, enabling them to increase their credit. On top of that the government decided to introduce a number of special anti-poverty measures via these groups, since this is where the poorest women can be found. Group members are given a free gas burner if they meet together for a whole year, for instance. Cooking with gas is good for the environment because it saves wood, but for the poor women it also saves time – time they can then use in a productive way.

Because of the measures taken by the state government, the number of women's groups in Andhra Pradesh has skyrocketed. According to official statistics there are now about 300,000 self-help groups active throughout the state, involving about 4 million women. If you assume each woman belongs to a household of five, that means one-third of the 65 million population of Andhra Pradesh is involved in this movement. The self-help women's movement in other parts of India is not as big (a total of 5 million more women are involved), but the number of women's groups is growing quickly all across the country.

A new impulse for the women's groups came in the form of a recent decision made by the Reserve Bank of India. All Indian commercial banks are required by law to issue 40 percent of their loans to so-called "priority groups": the landless, marginal farmers and microbusinesses. In other words, the banks are expected to make a contribution to the economic development of India. Traditionally this legal obligation has been a substantial loss item for banks, which are used to having to cancel between 40 and 50 percent of their credit portfolios. And the legal obligation doesn't have much of an impact either. Bank branches are located in every third village of India. Each branch can serve an average of 15,000 households, yet less than five percent of the loans issued to the informal sector come from the banks.

In 1996 the reserve bank decided that bank loans issued to the women's groups were to qualify as compulsory "priority loans." At first the banks paid no attention. Considering their negative experience with priority loans, they didn't think much of the idea of taking an even greater risk – as they saw it – to issue loans to the poorest women of India, who certainly wouldn't be creditworthy.

Yet a microcredit revolution took place in India, via the self-help groups. And that success is built on the work of one man.

I meet Vijay Mahajan early one morning as we step into a car together in Hyderabad, preparing to spend the whole day visiting villages in rural Andhra Pradesh. We need an hour to make our way through the chaotic, smoking traffic of the city – the sixth Indian city with over a million people after Calcutta, Delhi, Bombay, Madras and Bangalore. Once out of the urban centre we pass a gigantic film-studio complex, recently erected by a rich Indian to compete with the home of the great Indian film industry, "Bollywood" near Bombay. But according to reports, the completely furnished sets are regularly used as decors for Western films.

It takes a great deal of time to travel short distances in the countryside. The asphalt roads are used for all kinds of traffic. Oxcarts, scooters, bicyclists, loaded buses and decorated trucks: The road is a multi-coloured festival where you're forced to travel with the appropriate mixture of bravura and deference. Bravura if you're stronger. Deference if you're weaker. As the festival passes by we have time for Mahajan's life story.

He studied at India's leading school of management in Ahmedabad. With his diploma in his pocket, the road to the business world lay open to him. He began his first job at Philips, active in India since before the Second World War. But at Philips he didn't find the social challenge he was looking for to help his country advance. After four years he gave up his multinational career. He studied agrarian economics for a year in the United States and then travelled to the wide-open spaces of rural India. Twenty years later we're doing the same thing; in all these years Mahajan hasn't done anything else. At first he made these trips in traditional clothing with a beard and long hair. "My family almost disowned me, but my wife continued to believe in me," he recalls with a smile. He set up a non-profit organization, PRADAN, for rural development in the state of Rajasthan.

In his work in the countryside, Mahajan (who now dresses like a "Philips manager") discovered the importance of credit for the development of microbusinesses. So he set up BASIX in Hyderabad in 1996. BASIX is now the first and only Indian microfinancing institution that has permission to operate as a bank and to manage savings in a limited number of regions.

With BASIX, Mahajan is also devoting himself to issuing credit to women's groups to increase their clout. At a certain point, BASIX was the largest lender to women's groups in all of India. "I'm enormously attracted to the community model of these groups," Mahajan says. "They govern themselves. They're owned by the women. Any profits that are made with savings and loans are for the women themselves. There are signs of economic democracy and financial decentralization." In these respects the self-help groups differ substantially from the lending groups that many microfinancing institutions customarily use for the issuing of credit. The self-help groups manage their own money all by themselves.

To strengthen the movement of women's groups further, Mahajan lobbied intensively among the commercial banks within the organization of Indian microfinancing institutions called Sa-Dhan, which he also founded. He pressured these banks to issue loans to the groups as well.

At first the banks hesitated but finally they gave in. That was because BASIX could demonstrate that the women's groups have an almost-perfect repayment record. With the help of the reserve bank's liberalized priority regulation, the banks finally mustered the necessary nerve. After all, it was harder to get any worse than the usual loss of almost half of their credit portfolios. It's been a great success. Since 1999, more than 400 commercial Indian banks, working through 17,000 branches, issued credit amounting to $200 million to the women's groups, with a repayment percentage of at least 95 percent. The banks are enthusiastic. Never before had they found a priority sector to which they could lend money with so much success. At the same time, the flow of credit to the women's groups gave an enormous boost to the development of the countryside.

The $200 million u.s. in loans that the banks have given to 400,000 groups and about 6 million women since 1999 is significantly higher than the total credit issued by microfinancing institutions. All the Indian microfinancing institutions together have issued $80 million in microcredit. An incidental advantage for the women's groups is that the banks charge market interest for their loans, and that rate is approximately half the rate that the microfinancing institutions are forced to charge to cover their higher costs. The banks can charge market interest because they profit from the fact that India has the greatest number of banks per capita in the world. In addition, the women's groups have become more organized to strengthen their position. Several villages may join together in a federation, and the federation, which represents 1,500 women or more, serves as the contact group for the bank. For the banks, that's a very efficient way to work.

For Mahajan, the rapid increase in loans by commercial banks to women's groups is not a threat to microfinancing institutions such as his own basix. He points first of all to the gigantic challenge of the fight against poverty in India, where almost 400 million people are living under the official poverty line. The annual credit need of the approximately 75 million households is estimated at more than $130 u.s. per household. That means the total demand for microcredit is $10 billion. Says Mahajan, "In a market like this, you can't speak of competition. We need all the methods and institutions we can get to reach our goal – victory over poverty."

Despite his enthusiasm about the success of the women's groups and the loans issued by the banks, Mahajan also sees dangers. The banks are so greedy that the women's groups are not always formed with the necessary attention and care. Some bank employees are given to pulling a few women together in a group, issuing a loan and continuing to the next village. "It's not surprising that the repayment conduct of such groups will be poorer. That causes the banks to return to their old prejudice concerning the extending of credit to the poorest people, and then we're back where we started," says Mahajan.

Successful women's groups are often formed with the support of non-profit organizations. An employee of such a group brings the women together and helps them get organized. The women have lots of questions to answer. Why are we getting together? Where? How do we choose our leaders? How do we save? What do we do if someone doesn't save, or doesn't save enough? And especially: What are we saving for? What do we want to accomplish?

When the women together find answers, it creates not only a tightly knit group but one that serves a broader purpose than just saving and granting each other credit. Such a process can easily take two to three years. Experience also shows that a self-help group in the start-up phase needs from 15 to 20 days of training by a staff member of a non-profit organization. That costs about 10,000 rupees ($220 U.S.). The banks do not cover these costs. So launching the women's groups requires donor subsidies – in contrast with the loans from independent microfinancing institutions. But if that start-up phase is successfully completed, the women's groups are independent and self-supporting as well.

At the initiative of Vijay Mahajan, a special organization was set up in Andhra Pradesh to support the development of women's groups. Andhra Pradesh Mahila Abhivruddhi Society (APMAS) is under the leadership of the energetic C.S. Reddy. It's striking how common it is to see development work in India led by highly educated, intellectual, socially committed elite. Reddy, like Mahajan, and Kumar, could have found a job with Unilever, Philips or the Indian giant Tata.

Reddy storms into the room after being on the road for hours. He's visited villages in the most remote area of Andhra Pradesh, about 500 kilometres from the capital city of Hyderabad. He also went with local government officials to the village of Venkatrayachevruv. Living in that village are 100 families that are among the poorest in India. Within the past five years the women have organized themselves into groups. They want to buy 10 milk buffalo. The village is located on the route of a dairy factory, so the women stand a good chance of earning extra income. But 10 buffalo cost 80,000 rupees ($1,760), so that doesn't work. Branches of banks that could issue loans to the group don't exist in that remote district, so the women can't make more rapid headway.

"Don't think they let it go at that," says Reddy. "They really let us have it: 'We've been saving for five years because the state government told us to. But where are our loans? We want buffalo so we can sell the milk. Why does the teacher for our children only come two days a week?' These women are demanding action."

The increasing self-confidence among women is a clear result of the microcredit revolution. This is apparent among the Indian women's groups, but it's also true of the lending groups with which microcredit institutions work – in India and in other countries. Kumar puts it quite simply: "If you leave poverty behind, recognition and self-confidence come automatically." The examples are plentiful. Women who never learned to read or write are able to keep their daughters at school longer. They're more conscious of the number of children they conceive: "If I get pregnant now, I won't be able to work so hard and we won't be able to get a new loan."

Research shows that the use of family planning among the women of Grameen Bank is twice as widespread as the average figure for Bangladesh. "Why is that?" says Muhammad Yunus. "We're a bank, not a family planning institute. But it works like this: If people start taking life decisions into their own hands, they also start thinking about the size of their families." And the hygiene habits of Grameen families are better than in other Bengali families, too.

Interestingly enough, men see their wives' development as positive. This was the conclusion of a study conducted by the United Nations Development Program, UNDP, with regard to SHARE: "The fact that women regularly provide extra income is greatly appreciated by the men. That is why they do not object to the side effects. It seems that men are more able to discuss financial spending with their wives, and there is a greater tendency to include women in decision-making in general." Another observation from the report: Domestic violence against women decreases. The women themselves ascribe that to their increased value in economic terms. And widows and abandoned women feel safer. The women's groups clearly provide their members with mutual support.

Ultimately the emergence of women has political consequences as well. Muhammad Yunus called on all the women in rural Bangladesh to let themselves be heard in the 1996 elections. Because of that call, the turnout for Bengali women was an unprecedented 76 percent. And partly due to the massive women's turnout, the support for a fundamentalist Islamic party – which had ties to the Afghan Taliban – was virtually eliminated.

C.S. Reddy of APMAS praises the leadership skills shown by women in the Indian women's groups. "The management qualities, the organizational abilities, the negotiation techniques – it's phenomenal how effective and practical these often-illiterate women are in operation. The women's groups have released an enormous amount of energy." He chuckles as he tells about how women's groups even carry their government contracts with them to the market. If some road has to be mended and the government calls for tenders, members put their names down for the delivery of the necessary sand. "The women don't shrink from bribing officials. Non-profit organizations strongly disapprove, but the women say, 'That's the way we do things here. We wanted to get that work.'"

Signs that women are advancing are abundant. More and more women in India are running for office in representative bodies. Thirty-three percent of the seats have always been reserved for women by law, but in practise that usually means women were sent by their husbands to be elected. Now women are increasingly offering themselves for office on their own and with their own agendas. Reddy says, "There aren't any more 'stupid' women serving as mouthpieces for their husbands. These are 'real' women who want something." He pauses for a moment. "We're seeing a jewel," he says. "The very poorest women are standing for office... and they're getting elected."

Julia and David

In her mouth there's a flash of gold teeth – a sign of prosperity. She walks confidently through the rooms of the shop where carpenters and woodcutters are working on furniture in various stages of production. Massive wooden frames are skilfully being worked into couches, cabinets, buffets and chairs. Couches are upholstered with colourful fabrics. The furniture workshop owned and run by Julia Zacarias and her husband David Guisbert, on one of the steep mountain slopes above the Bolivian capital of La Paz, now employs 15 people. When they started the company more than 20 years ago, David worked more or less on his own, sometimes helped by a single assistant.

Twenty years ago the company expanded enormously after Julia and David took out their first loan from the Bolivian microfinancing institution Centro de Fomento a Iniciativas Económicas (FIE). With that loan of $5,000 (some loans in Bolivia are provided directly in u.s. dollars) they purchased a power saw. Before the machine arrived, it took David a week to make a couch – completely by hand. With the machine he makes two couches in 10 days. Production increased even further with the hiring of more employees. Today, the total monthly output from the shop includes 25 living room sets (two couches, a chair, a coffee table and two side tables) and eight dining room sets (eight chairs, a table and a buffet). The gross income is at least $5,000 a month and the profit $1,500, more than enough to make the monthly payments to FIE and live comfortably.

Because of the successful growth of the company, the couple's five children are able to attend private school. And whereas Julia and David began their married lives in a rented room, they now live in a house they built themselves, where all the children have a room of their own. "And we have a kitchen," says Julia proudly. But David still works seven days a week from 7 in the morning to 8 at night. That's because there are always new goals. The nearby showroom/shop – where one of their daughters holds sway – is bulging at the seams. Work is now being done on a new house, with separate living room and dining room showrooms on the ground floor.

In the past 15 years Julia and David have taken out increasingly larger loans from FIE, and paid them all back. In 2001 they reached a new pinnacle: a permanent $40,000 credit line. This enables them to purchase wood and fabric, which is imported to La Paz at irregular times, in large amounts. With that credit line and 15 employees, Julia and David's business has outgrown the microsector.

CHAPTER 4

The Price of Money

Microcredit is expensive. The interest charged by microfinancing institutions varies between 20 and 40 percent – the rate is usually at least 10 percentage points above the interest that established banks charge their customers and sometimes much more. The institutions differ from banks in that they don't open a teller's window for receiving potential customers. Employees from microfinancing institutions go out to visit their customers. That requires quite a bit of effort in the slums of a huge underdeveloped metropolis, and travel across a vast expanse of countryside takes a great deal of time.

So the number of customers that an employee can serve is limited. An employee of Grameen Bank in Bangladesh has an average of 200 customers. At the κ-Rep Bank in Kenya that average is around 400 borrowers per employee. An ordinary bank, by contrast, serves thousands of account holders with a handful of personnel. That's why personnel costs at microfinancing institutions are so much higher. And they've got to earn back those higher costs by charging interest to their customers. One-third to half of the interest rate at microfinancing institutions is spent on employee salaries.

The high interest levels are a contentious subject in the world of microcredit. It seems almost unreasonable to make the poor of the world pay extra for their small loans. After all, isn't it wonderful that they take out loans and pay them off? That this kind of development aid isn't just a one-shot deal, but that it's always properly returned so it can be used again? If ever there was a place for interest-free credit, this is it. Right?

This point of view is quite understandable, but it runs up against the need for microfinancing institutions to run cost-effective operations. If the institutions don't make a profit, they can't attract any capital or loans with which to issue new microcredit. In other words: If the poor entrepreneur pays the price for the money, institutions are able to offer him loans. If he doesn't, the institutions can't survive and he becomes dependent on donors who make "free" money available to him. Such money is never enough to meet the total demand for small-scale loans. Even more important is the fact that going the "donor route," discussed in chapter 1, is not a sustainable solution for microfinancing in the developing world.

In La Paz, the otherwise friendly and easy-going Fernando Prado, director of DAI, raises his voice when he talks about an initiative of the European Union (EU) to offer microcredit in Bolivia at lower interest rates: "European parliamentarians take this kind of initiative because they think the interest is too high. But by doing this they threaten the continuity of local microfinancing institutions. Those local institutions are crucial for the entrepreneurs. One fine day the other parliamentarians of the EU will stop giving money for microcredit because they've got other priorities. Then the entrepreneur will be without any credit at all, because the local independent microfinancing institutions will have disappeared. They will have been driven away by the subsidies. The most expensive loan is the loan that doesn't exist. Naturally everyone wants an interest rate that's as low as possible. But even more important than that are viable institutions that can cover their costs and keep pursuing their mission to fight poverty."

Kumar of SHARE in Hyderabad feels compelled to charge non-cost-effective interest rates in some villages. He does this to compete with the rates charged by microcredit institutions financed by Western donors – rates of 10 percent, for instance. "That's the wrong kind of competition. But if I can afford to suffer a loss in a single village, I will. Later the donor institutions will be gone, and SHARE will have been able to maintain its clientele," says Kumar.

The experiences of Prado and Kumar illustrate the fatal influence that good Western intentions can have on the development of microfinancing. But the most important argument for a realistic interest rate is not financial. A real price also means real value. Ramirez of FIE in La Paz says, "If you give someone a loan, you are expressing appreciation for that person and for what he or she does. If it turns out there's a subsidy in that loan, the sense of appreciation is also reduced. Charity creeps in, with the accompanying relationship of dependence. When poor entrepreneurs are taken seriously and really permitted to participate it gives them an enormous boost. That's 90 percent of the effect."

Ramirez's point of view seems to have been confirmed by indications that subsidized interest rates negatively influence the repayment conduct of borrowers. In El Salvador, Save the Children charged the extremely low interest of three percent per year but recorded the abominable repayment score of 52 percent. There are comparable examples. Prado of DAI says subsidized interest rates create the impression that a gift is involved that doesn't have to be paid back. Such rates also stimulate inefficient investment.

The almost-perfect repayment conduct of small, poor entrepreneurs suggests that the interest is not too high. Almost all microfinancing institutions score repayment percentages above 95 percent, often above 97 percent. Studies even show the scores of the poorest entrepreneurs as relatively the best. Even though they don't have a lot of money, their enormous desire to enable their children to have a better future gives the women the drive they need to comply carefully with the terms of repayment. They want to go further and they do, and the interest doesn't stand in their way.

Interest doesn't weigh so heavily on these small-scale entrepreneurs because they reap high yields with microcredit. The average yield is about 100 percent. In other words, entrepreneurs double the value of their possessions – and the exceptional 400 percent is not uncommon. The interest microfinancing institutions charge varies from 20 to 40 percent. The profit for the entrepreneur amounts to his yield minus the interest, always about 80 percent. So he can easily afford to pay the interest.

The following three examples bear that out.

In the first, an Indian woman wants to generate extra income. She borrows 7,000 rupees ($152 u.s.) from a microfinancing institution and buys a milk buffalo. She has 50 weeks to pay back the loan, along with interest of 24 percent – a total of 8,680 rupees ($188), 174 rupees ($3.75) per week, 34 rupees (75 cents) of which is interest. She has no other costs. The buffalo eats grass in the village. Each day the buffalo produces three litres of milk, which the woman sells for 15 rupees (33 cents) per litre at the market. Her daily yield is therefore 45 rupees ($1). Each week she earns 315 rupees ($6.85). She therefore has an extra income of 315 – 174 = 141 rupees, or $3 – a profit of 141 percent. After 50 weeks she satisfies the obligations to her microfinancing institution. The next year, her income from the milk buffalo increases to 315 rupees a week, an additional profit of 123 percent for a total of 264 percent. (Things will go a bit differently in actual practise. After a year, a milk buffalo undergoes a dry period. The woman will overcome that problem by purchasing a second buffalo, etc.)

In the second, a rickshaw driver in Bangladesh is too poor to buy his own rickshaw. Every day he hires a rickshaw from a clever extortionist at eight taka (12 cents u.s.) a day. That's more than 2,900 taka ($44) a year. For the same money he could buy his own second-hand rickshaw. He obtains a loan of 2,900 taka from a microfinancing institution. He has to pay back this money in 50 weeks, along with 20 percent interest – a total of 3,480 taka ($1,587), or more than nine taka a day, one and a half taka of which is interest. That's more than he's used to paying for hiring a rickshaw, but after a year he'll be an independent operator and his income will skyrocket.

In a third, a Bolivian woman takes out a loan of 500 bolivianos ($62) to purchase five piglets. She has to pay off the loan in six months, plus interest of 24 percent annually. That means she has to pay back 560 bolivianos ($70) in monthly payments of 93 bolivianos ($12) – 10 bolivianos of which is interest. Other than this she has very few expenses: The pigs eat mostly household scraps and plants growing around the woman's hut. After six months, the woman can sell the five pigs for at least 1,000 bolivianos – a profit of 100 percent. The monthly repayment comes from additional household income – a typical example of saving for the future.

In all three examples, the interest plays a minor role in the figures. The woman with the buffalo had no extra income before, and now she does – which helps fight the poverty of her family. The rickshaw driver is on his way to being an independent operator at a price that's just a bit higher than the rental he's used to paying – which he would have had to pay for the rest of his life if it had not been for the loan. The woman with the five pigs actually saves 500 bolivianos in six months, on which she pays 60 bolivianos interest. In this way she might save to buy a piece of land for a house or for agriculture.

The poor entrepreneurs regard the interest they pay as the price of money. Before the arrival of microfinancing institutions in the cities and villages, entrepreneurs could still obtain money. There were always people who supplied credit: loan sharks – moneylenders. But money obtained from that source was, and still is (besides microfinancing institutions, loan sharks are still an important source of financing for small entrepreneurs in developing countries), considerably more expensive. Ten percent per month is cheap for a loan shark; five percent per day is not unusual. That is to say: With the arrival of microfinancing institutions, the price of money for poor entrepreneurs plummeted.

On top of that is the ease with which microfinancing institutions issue credit. At the Bolivian FIE, the total procedure – from the first request to the payment of the loan – takes a maximum of five days. A subsequent loan is even issued within three days. That speed is of critical importance in the market, with the rapid terms of credit within which microbusinesses function. In ordinary banks – insofar as they represent an accessible alternative for informal entrepreneurs – a loan application requires an extensive bureaucratic procedure with a series of official documents: passports, declarations, notaries – all things that hardly exist in the informal economy of poor entrepreneurs in developing countries, if they exist at all. Such a procedure can easily take a month at least, and for microbusiness entrepreneurs that means watching their chances go down the drain once again.

The informal market consists of incidents and irregular supply. Say a dealer shows up today with a parcel of wood that's of interest to a furniture maker. It's hard to say when the next parcel is coming, if at all. In such circumstances, convenience counts far more than the interest rate – which is why loan sharks have always been able to make a good living.

This doesn't alter the fact that the entrepreneurs might be able to leave their poverty behind sooner if they had to pay less interest. As far as this is concerned, two possibilities are promising. First of all, microfinancing institutions can lower their costs. Economizing on personnel costs is no option, considering the nature of microcredit financing. But the institutions can save money by attracting more savings. Many institutions now borrow money for loans from commercial banks. They pay interest on this money, and the rate is easily 10 to 12 percent. Savers are satisfied with half that: five to six percent. So attracting savings is clearly a cheaper way for microfinancing institutions to finance loans. And the institutions can use that "profit" to lower their interest rates. This option is very attractive because many microfinancing institutions are eager to manage their customers' savings – or in countries where that is not yet possible to wait for new regulations that allow for it.

The increasing consideration ordinary banks are giving microfinancing allows for a second option for lowering interest. In Bolivia and Kenya, for example, urban banks are finding ways to earn money from poor entrepreneurs through microlending – while maintaining their normal interest rates. This has to do with the concentration of potential customers in certain locations and with the fact that the poor entrepreneurs have become familiar with microfinancing. The potential customers are entrepreneurs, moreover, so they're interested in competition. If a bank were to open a branch in their neighbourhoods today and to focus specifically on them as potential clientele, they would be inclined to walk in. In the past – before the arrival of microfinancing institutions – the threshold of a bank was something that the poor simply could not cross.

In other words, the arrival of established banks in this new market is helping to lower microcredit interest rates. But that option exists only in places where microfinancing has taken hold in the community and where there is a certain minimal market volume. This is also borne out by the experience of commercial banks in the Indian countryside. Those banks now lend extensively to women's groups at the going interest rates (see chapter 3). This can take place quite efficiently because the women's groups organize themselves into federations in which 1,500 women or more are represented. Such a scale makes it possible for the banks to extend loans at the standard rate.

The path to the millions of poor people who still have no access to microfinancing can only be cleared by microfinancing institutions – with their higher costs. That pioneering work – searching for customers and familiarizing them with microfinancing – is too expensive for banks, which operate with market interest rates. Microcredit continues to be expensive. But that doesn't have to be a big problem. In order to write this book I visited about 25 microentrepreneurs in Kenya, Uganda, Bolivia and India. At each spot we engaged in extensive discussions about their wishes, challenges and problems. I've heard plenty of complaints: about the absence of electricity or water, for example, or the inconvenience of bad roads. But not one entrepreneur complained about how high the interest was. If I asked about it, they would laugh and talk about the rates the loan sharks charge in the market. It was a small-scale field investigation with a clear conclusion: The "high" interest – the price of money – is no problem for small entrepreneurs in the struggle to end their own poverty.

Veneranda and Bonface

Kawangware is the human version of an anthill, where everyone lives in chaos with an apparently clear-cut mission. Women hawking their wares – *mama mbogas* – sell vegetables along the roadside, the sand having triumphed over the asphalt long ago. Charcoal dealers trudge along carrying canisters. Delivery buses – *matatas* – with too many passengers inside negotiate the potholes in the road, travelling a zigzag course.

It's winter in Kenya, and the temperature in this slum at the edge of Nairobi is perhaps 20 degrees Fahrenheit. Clouds cover the sun, and people walk about in wool sweaters. On a street corner a man is deep-frying a kind of egg roll in a large pan filled with oil. Behind him is the blue façade of his wife's little shop. The "shop" has a floor surface of maybe four square metres (44 square feet), but it is the pride of Veneranda and Bonface.

Veneranda used to sell vegetables and charcoal along the roadside, just like the other *mama mbogas*. That was until 1999, when she was granted a loan of 5,000 shillings ($60 U.S.) from the Kenyan microfinancing bank K-Rep. With that money Veneranda rented her shop and invested in a wider assortment of merchandise: lentils, rice, sugar, salt, oil, flour and soap, but also a few lollipops, a pack of chewing gum, a bottle of cola and a roll of toilet paper. Veneranda, with her little roadside stand, used to have a daily turnover of 300 shillings (20 cents). The daily turnover of her shop now amounts to an average of 10 times that amount: 3,000 shillings ($2). The "profit" goes to their four children, who now can go to school every day. In the past the children sometimes went a month without going to school because there wasn't enough money to pay school fees. And the quality of the daily meals has vastly improved. Now Veneranda can spend 150 or even 200 shillings (10 or 15 cents) a day on food, whereas she used to spend no more than 50 – about 3 cents u.s.

Veneranda and Bonface proudly invite us to their house right behind the shop. It has an area less than 20 square metres or 300 square feet with a "kitchen," a "living room" and – behind a curtain – a "bedroom": for six people. Veneranda has now negotiated two larger loans with k-Rep. Everything is invested in expanding the stock of merchandise, because, "If you say you don't have something, the people don't come back," says Veneranda. Her last loan of 40,000 shillings ($480) has been paid back. She's looking forward to her next loan. The shop needs shelves along one wall so the products can be displayed better. That investment will mean taking out yet another loan.

CHAPTER 5

Happy but Dissatisfied

I'm typing these lines on a laptop in a remote village at the heart of Sri Lanka. My mud hut, like the other mud huts in Ulpotha, has no electricity. The last pole in the electricity grid is kilometres away. Yet here I am, peacefully writing without a worry in the world on this instrument of modern technology. My computer quietly hums on without high-tension cables because it's powered by a solar panel. This breakthrough to clean, sustainable economy is not taking place in the wealthy West; here the developing world is leading the way. In the past 10 years, solar panels have become increasingly popular in many developing countries. There are thousands of remote villages in the warm, sunny parts of the world that will never be part of the national electricity grid. It's too expensive to lay the cables because so few people would be served. It doesn't pay, the governments conclude, so they don't bother.

But solar panels don't require a gigantic investment. For 30,000 Sri Lankan rupees (about $300) you have a system that can keep five light bulbs burning in a hut. And there's power left over for my laptop. No more nasty smell. No more black scorched walls. No fire hazard. No carbon dioxide emissions. Progress on every front. But in my village, $300 is a lot of money. So my host went to the Sri Lankan microcredit institution Sarvodaya Economic Enterprise Development Services (SEEDS) – part of the Sarvodaya movement, which has been fighting poverty and working on behalf of socio-economic development in Sri Lanka for 40 years. He was one of the 20,000 Sri Lankans to purchase a solar panel within the past three years with loans from SEEDS. A total of 30,000 such systems have been bought in the last 10 years. In other words: The growing popularity of solar panels in Sri Lanka didn't really take off until microcredit became available.

The solar panel on my hut's roof of woven palm leaves is an example of the opportunities microfinancing offers for economic development. But progress is not always so easy to assess. The relationship between the individual economic progress of microcredit borrowers and the economic development taking place in their countries is difficult to determine. Is the goal of microfinancing institutions – fighting poverty – being reached? Are we looking at substantial progress and development over the long term? It's hard to answer these questions because the statistical bureaus are no help – as the following example illustrates.

A few days ago I was in Bentota, a village on the west coast of Sri Lanka, riding in a scooter rickshaw. Kapila, the driver, was very proud of his brand-new red vehicle. He had recently bought the rickshaw with a loan from a microfinancing institution. The rickshaw was made by Bajaj, an Indian manufacturer that is No. 1 in the production of scooter rickshaws. Bajaj is an established Indian enterprise that publishes figures incorporated in the calculation of the national Indian income. Kapila's purchase has an effect on the official economic figures: The Bajaj turnover has gone up. The bookkeeping of the Sri Lankan importer of scooter rickshaws has a place in the Sri Lankan statistics. But that's where the official effect of Kapila's purchase of a new rickshaw – and of the microcredit that made it possible for him to make this purchase – comes to a halt. There are other effects, however.

Kapila used to work on the staff of a hotel. He had a fixed salary. As a self-employed operator he makes more. But this shows up in the national income as a negative development: The official hotel salary that got counted is replaced by a freelance income in the informal sector that doesn't get counted – assuming no one is hired to replace him. Kapila keeps no records and pays no taxes. It isn't that he doesn't want to, but registering as a self-employed entrepreneur in a country like Sri Lanka – where the births are haphazardly registered and people often can't even prove who they are – is so complicated that it's impossible. Kapila's situation improves. Because of his higher income, the daily meals eaten by his family become more varied, and that benefits their resistance and health.

Kapila's wife now buys papayas and mangos more frequently from other women with informal roadside vegetable businesses – which they run without records. And their children can now attend the private – and better – school in the village. The figures from the school may be included in the national income. But the overall effect of Kapila's decision to become a self-employed entrepreneur won't really be evident until the next generation, when his children have found an even better future (in the formal sector?) thanks to their educations.

You won't be able to trace the progress of Kapila and his family – made possible thanks to microcredit – in the national income of Sri Lanka. Since most of their progress takes place in the informal sector, the national per capita income does not advance. This is the figure that ministers and policymakers want to see increasing because that's the kind of calculation they're used to. And because they're stuck in their ways, the effects – and thus the importance – of microcredit are often disputed. In turn, pioneers of microfinancing institutions are wary of claiming success for microcredit based on statistics. They point out that it takes more than loans to fight poverty.

The causal relationship between microcredit and the official economic figures is usually missing. If an informal microbusiness expands and hires more personnel, you never see it reflected in the employment statistics. Jane opens a beauty parlour in Nairobi. She's so successful that she's able to hire two additional hairdressers. Later she starts a hairdressing school and trains even more entrepreneurs, who start beauty parlours of their own and create more jobs (see Portrait viii). And the woman who hired Padma to work in her sari-edging business in a rural village in the Indian state of Andhra Pradesh doesn't have an official job (see Portrait vii). But more work comes in, thanks to microcredit, and that is a valuable contribution to the fight against poverty.

The quality of the investment is very important to the success of microcredit, of course. Lending in and of itself does not create economic opportunities. It only helps put entrepreneurs and their companies in a position to take advantage of any opportunities that might come along. In other words: Microcredit helps fight poverty if there are opportunities that can be exploited with the help of credit. But the most harrowing forms of poverty are beyond the reach of credit. On the other hand, Ramirez of FIE estimates that in Bolivia – one of the poorest countries in the world – "no more than five percent" of the poor are in such a state that microcredit cannot contribute to their development.

Many opportunities exist, but one problem is that poor entrepreneurs are often inclined to copy their neighbours. In the village of Nagasonkola on the road from Kampala to the north of Uganda, I saw 10 women sitting side by side with practically identical vegetable stands. It was a small village and there was little traffic on the road. Under such circumstances, not all can be successful. This is a phenomenon you see in many places. In Kawangware, the Nairobi slum, you can hardly walk a metre without stumbling over a charcoal dealer. I only ran into one who had seen a really fresh opportunity *and* seized it.

John Muigai became a dealer in real estate – and incredibly rich. I've never seen anyone succeed so well through microcredit (see Portrait IV). Muigai is concerned about the way poor entrepreneurs tend to copy each other "Soon you'll have more dealers than ordinary citizens in Kenya," he comments. Mutua of K-Rep in Nairobi adds, "You see little innovation. Hundreds of women have the same little vegetable businesses. No one realizes that you might be able to package those vegetables."

Generally speaking, investing in production is more effective than extending microcredit to dealers and service businesses. That's why the Bolivian FIE issued loans exclusively to production companies at first. But it abandoned this practise because for the poor, small trading businesses are often a first step towards entrepreneurship. That explains the excess of vegetable and charcoal businesses. That explains the need for innovation. That explains why so much has to happen before poverty in the world is conquered for good.

It's often difficult to draw a direct connection between microcredit and the increase in the recipient's income. In the case of Kapila and his scooter rickshaw, that connection – informal in any case – is discernible. Often progress is evident in the increased number of possessions and their value, although the income from the microbusiness doesn't change at all.

In 1997 the World Bank undertook an extensive study of the effect of microcredit issued by the Grameen Bank in Bangladesh. The promising conclusion was that the Grameen Bank had succeeded in pulling one-third of its borrowers out of poverty and in helping one-third to such an extent that they were able to climb just beyond the poverty line. Every month, 10,000 Bengali families cross the poverty line. Those conclusions were not based on income statistics, however, but on the fact that Grameen borrowers are better off than other families in Bangladesh in terms of nutrition, child mortality, sanitary facilities, use of birth control and availability of safe drinking water.

A study of the granting of credit by SHARE, carried out in 2001 by CASHPOR, the Malaysian network for financial services to the very poor, found that three out of four customers of this microfinancing institution "experience a significant reduction in their poverty." At the beginning of the study, CASHPOR called the vast majority of SHARE's customers "very poor," and when the study was completed they placed only seven percent of customers in this category. The greatest change was the addition of at least one new source of income to the household: a buffalo, a sewing machine, etc. Kumar says, "Microcredit is one of the most powerful instruments for fighting poverty. We succeed in raising the poor to a level at which ordinary banks can take over. Five percent of our borrowers have already become customers of a bank and now borrow more than 50,000 rupees ($1,000)." And with reference to Bolivia, economist Paul Mosle wrote in an appendix to the *World Development Report 2000*, "Microcredit is making a substantial contribution to the reduction of poverty." And: "The costs of fighting poverty by means of microcredit are much lower than by means of other social expenditures."

Indeed, poor Bolivia is the most interesting country when it comes to evaluating the effect of microcredit. It has only 8 million inhabitants and a relatively large number of microfinancing institutions. Nowhere has microfinancing touched more people or gone more deeply into society. In fact, in Bolivian cities the reach is total. All the urban poor who wanted credit for their microbusinesses have been able to get it since 1985. Most poor entrepreneurs can even choose between institutions. If microcredit really works, you ought to be able to see it in the Bolivian cities (the sparsely populated countryside is an entirely different story).

The first hitch is that the informal sector in poor Bolivia makes up the greater part of the economy. So for an evaluation of the effect of microcredit it's pointless to consider the development of the national per-capita income. Nevertheless, Franz Gómez Soto of the Superintendencia de Bancos y Entidades Financieras, the institution that monitors banking and financial institutions, is convinced of "a certain success." Microfinancing's clientele prove it, he says. The 10 ordinary banks of Bolivia, operating for decades, together have 160,000 customers. Eight microfinancing institutions, in existence for less than 20 years, together have 175,000 customers. In addition, the percentage of overdue payments is *much* lower among the microfinancing institutions. Gómez also points to the official figures indicating that poverty in Bolivia has been reduced in the last 10 years. Back then, more than seven out of 10 Bolivians lived under the poverty line. Now it's six. But the definition of what constitutes the poverty line is a subject of extensive debate.

Ramirez of FIE doesn't search the statistics for proof of success. In the early 1990s her customers who manufactured clothing, and who had received their first loans in 1985, cautiously began exporting their wares to Brazil, Argentina and Peru. They did this through informal channels – smuggling – in small amounts. Even so, these were the signs of success that Ramirez was looking for. "Usually it's poor people producing things for other poor people. We've got to break free of this. That's why exporting is so important," she says. The tragedy was that the success was almost immediately suffocated by an economic recession in Bolivia's three neighbouring countries, causing them to close their borders and to guard them energetically.

Shortly thereafter Bolivia itself fell into recession, which has now been persisting for five years. The informal sector had to absorb that recession – because when the official jobs are gone, people take refuge in the informal sector. The informal sector was barely able to process the enormous influx, which had its effect on the development of microbusinesses. Yet the average loan issued by FIE is increasing each year. This means credit needs are increasing, and more is being invested. In 1998 the average FIE loan was $838; right now it's about $1,200. And Ramirez adds, "We have customers who borrowed $100 15 years ago and are now borrowing $5,000."

And there's a hopeful new trend: Established Bolivian fabrics companies recently began farming out part of their production to microbusinesses. In this way those microbusinesses are "admitted" to the established economy. But poverty in Bolivia is by no means a thing of the past. "When I'm feeling cynical," says Ramirez, "I say we've avoided social unrest because people were kept busy paying off their loans. When I'm feeling more positive, I see that our customers have changed. Their children go to school, which they didn't do before. [Customers] have possessions like a sewing machine or a transport bus. They've added a new room to their house. Their living conditions and health have improved. They're better dressed. They save more money. They have more self-respect. And they now have a better understanding of financial affairs. In 1985 we said, 'We're going to issue loans to people who have no access to credit.' We can't say that any more, because everyone in the cities of Bolivia can get credit. On television you see adverts from banks aimed at the lowest income groups. All these are steps in the right direction. You can't evaluate microfinancing from income growth alone; you don't suddenly see the roads packed with Mercedes."

Ramirez sees progress in terms of a broader trend. "In 1985 you only saw white faces [the elite of European origin] in the bank. If you go to a bank today, you see all colours. And about 15 years ago the only people who studied with the whites at the university were a few privileged representatives of native population groups. Now it's the other way round. A bridge has been built. I'm not saying that this was done by microcredit, but these developments do go hand in hand. It's a social movement."

Possessions grow sooner than incomes. That's the general tendency in poor circles and has everything to do with culture: People are accustomed to a certain way of life. If things are going better with their businesses, they'll send their children to school or to a better school, and they may spend more on their daily meals, but you won't see big differences in the way they spend their money. What does clearly increase is the value of their possessions. This also has to do with the fact that family and business overlap. You often notice that a business with a new microcredit loan does not appear to undergo any kind of change. The same man and woman are working, there's no new staff, no higher income. But the family has bought a piece of land on which they're growing their own food; buffalo provide milk and extra income, and the condition of the house has improved. The loan hasn't been invested in the business but into the family household.

SOMED in Uganda maintains lists of their borrowers' possessions. When the first loan is applied for, that list may say "bicycle, furniture, radio, temporary house." When subsequent loans are sought, the list will be expanded: "a fan, television, a *permanent* house." Or perhaps a reed roof has been replaced by corrugated iron. This is how SOMED is able to determine – without complicated calculations – that two-thirds of its borrowers are making progress in their lives. Benjamin Byarugaba says, "I'm happy with that result, but I'm not satisfied. I want 100 percent of my customers to profit."

The challenge to SOMED customers living in thinly populated areas is the market. The Grameen Bank has discovered that borrowers in the heavily populated parts of Bangladesh become each other's customers. One woman sells milk and uses her income to become the customer of another woman, who sells firewood. It's Adam Smith at work: Value is created and so is a market for that value. Kumar sees the same thing taking place in India: "People who were used to walking dozens of kilometres a day to buy something can now get it in their own village. In 10 years I've never seen poor entrepreneurs unable to get rid of their products. There's always a market."

It's different in Africa. "In Bangladesh and India there's a customer for every pancake, but for my customers it's not so simple," says Byarugaba. SOMED customers travel from Masindi to Kampala to sell their pulp cane products. They take the vegetables and fruit they've grown to places where food is scarce. Or they raise flowers they can sell somewhere else. For these Ugandans the road to the market is a hard one and impedes progress.

If the market is close at hand, the absence of infrastructure can still stand in the way of progress. In the village of Ilapuram in Indian state of Andhra Pradesh, I saw farmer Deshaboina successfully improve the life of his family by purchasing milk buffalo, with the help of microcredit (also see Portrait 111). But Deshaboina could be successful because his village was 15 minutes by bicycle from the regional centre of Suryapet. Because there's a dairy store owned by a dairy co-operative, there's also a veterinarian working in the neighbourhood. Those are essential ingredients that determine the success of Deshaboina and his microcredit. A comparable farmer in a remote village without a vet and cold store nearby would never have been able to achieve the same success, even with the same loan. That farmer may have been able to do something different with his microcredit, but a lucrative investment in milk buffalo would not have been an option for him.

Knowledge also has a great deal to do with the success of microcredit. Not all buffalo owners succeed equally well, and these differences can often be traced to lack of knowledge and experience. Many farmers in the countryside still work as their forefathers did. They cultivate a single crop, which makes them unnecessarily vulnerable. Spreading the risk out over two or three crops offers them a greater prospect of success and of support from microfinancing institutions. BASIX of India organizes visits for less successful farm-

SMALL CHANGE

ers to their more successful colleagues so they can learn how to provide better care for their animals.

General technical support is of vital importance. Kumar of SHARE says, "Money alone isn't enough. Training is also necessary." Each SHARE borrower first undergoes a kind of "small business training."

"To turn people into entrepreneurs you have to offer them services," says Kumar. SHARE also organizes specific training programmes for groups – cattle breeders, say, or carpenters – led by experts. SOMED in Uganda also trains its customers in such skills as bookkeeping. Benjamin Byarugaba says, "Most people here are illiterate. They know nothing about bookkeeping. We have to do more to enable them to improve their lives."

Many microfinancing institutions began with this kind of broad approach – granting loans and providing technical support – but finally decided to concentrate on microfinancing. For FIE in Bolivia, training was initially a condition for a loan. Entrepreneurs would be given lessons for a month, mainly in bookkeeping. FIE discontinued that policy because of the aversion of the entrepreneurs and the realization that the institution was "turning the entrepreneurs into accountants."

It does make sense to provide specific training aimed at the needs of the entrepreneur. But such training is often too expensive for microfinancing institutions. Some microfinancing institutions see this as an opportunity to work with non-profit organizations. Technical support can then be financed by donor money while the microfinancing institutions remain self-supporting and independent. FIE and the K-Rep Bank in Kenya also continue to work with the non-profit organizations of the same name from which these institutions emerged. Financed by donor money, these organizations are active in areas that are not remunerative for the financial institutions. This has proven to be a fruitful form of co-operation and provides a new opportunity for the role of non-profit organizations in supporting the economy of the developing world. BASIX in India combines microfinancing and technical support in a specific, ingenious way. The institution attempts to bring different parties together to create favourable market conditions within a specific area from which as many people as possible can profit. This approach concentrates the "training energy" of BASIX for a maximum return.

For example: BASIX identified a dairy factory operating at only 10 percent of its full output. Too few farmers in the area had buffalo that could provide milk on a regular basis. So BASIX employees went out to the villages near the factory looking for farmers who would be willing to take out loans to invest in buffalo for milk production. The loans were then paid through the dairy co-operative, which subtracted the funds for BASIX from the funds to the farmers for the delivered milk. After a year and a half the factory was running at full capacity.

In another region, BASIX noticed that 90 percent of the farmers were raising peanuts. In such a situation, improvement can have an effect on large groups of people. All the farmers in the area delivered their peanuts to one factory, which produced peanut oil. But selling peanuts for direct consumption is much more lucrative. That option required a better quality of peanut, however. BASIX found a peanut company prepared to undertake a study to determine what kinds of measures would have to be taken by the farmers – better seed, fertilizing – to raise the quality of their peanuts. That company would then buy up the peanuts.

BASIX subsequently discovered that more was being paid for shelled peanuts than for unshelled, and that for 1,000 rupees ($20 U.S.) a machine could be purchased to do the shelling. Through carefully directed efforts and support from BASIX, these farmers now sell their peanuts for 17 rupees (32 cents U.S.) a kilo, whereas they previously got 10 rupees (20 cents) a kilo from the oil factory. This constitutes an important contribution to the economic progress in the region. BASIX provides a third of its loans this way, in co-operation with a company or government institution responsible for infrastructure or access to the market.

The examples of milk and peanut production from BASIX demonstrate that the success of microcredit can be significantly increased when supplemented with certain measures. Mahajan of BASIX says, "Microcredit is a necessary but insufficient condition for fighting poverty through the development of microbusinesses." Mutua of K-Rep Bank is of the same opinion. His bank finances a great many activities in the slums of Kawangware in Nairobi. "Our customers' turnover would triple if the government were to improve the road to Kawangware and guarantee safety in the area. Such measures have a much greater effect than we can reach with microcredit alone."

Indeed, in a beauty parlour in Kawangware I saw well-to-do women who were clearly from the prosperous centre of Nairobi. These women had taken the trouble of coming to the beauty parlour by travelling the neglected road. A better road and more safety would certainly bring more women like these to the low-priced hairdressers of Kawangware.

Who's going to build the infrastructure that will help the poor advance? You can't build roads or power stations with microcredit. But governments have no money. And when there was money, large-scale investments in developing countries have often yielded disappointing results. Mutua says, "It's wonderful that people can borrow and save. But the most important thing about microfinancing is the philosophy: Base the work on the actual situation of the poor, create institutions where the people are, and let the poor actively participate in their own development. You can adapt the same philosophy to health care, education and energy. So we shouldn't follow the point of view taken by the World Bank, which says that the energy sector should be privatized. That could lead to two competing giants who would never bring electricity to the remote villages. Following the pattern of microcredit, you can opt for micro-energy – with windmills and solar panels – and thus provide electricity to a village of 50 inhabitants. That's an alternative that works."

The same is true of health care. A few years ago the World Bank forced Kenya to stop subsidizing large public hospitals because it was too expensive. So poor people can no longer go to hospitals, and no alternative exists. K-Rep is now working on the creation of a new company that will open small clinics as well as offer medical insurance for the poor.

The same goes for schools. And for road maintenance. Indian women's groups were given a government commission to maintain the roads in their area. The Grameen Bank set up separate companies in mobile telephone systems, fish processing, textiles and dairy production to provide further support to the development of the poor. Such connections are based on the concepts of small-scale operations and involvement. It's a fundamental choice.

Structures are more important than money. A microfinancing institution – working independently, financed by the savings from the poor themselves and independent of donor funding – can ultimately play a very significant role in the fight against poverty, and this can work for economic development too.

In *Mainstreaming Microfinance* by Beth Rhyne, Bolivian President Gonzalo Sánchez de Lozada says, "People can make better decisions about investing their money than the state can do on their behalf. You can do a great deal more to end poverty if you give people the power to decide how they want to spend their money. You must treat the poor as the makers of their own economic development. It is arrogant to say that microcredit is only balm on the wound. You've got to be careful with attitudes like these. The undercurrents of economic activity are much more powerful than you can see from the surface. You cannot underestimate what people will do with their resources. Only now do we realize that it's the people who make a country rich."

Microcredit is a vital source of support in the process of development. All by itself it's already working small miracles, but coupled with a broader approach that effect can be intensified. The challenge is gigantic. In India alone the market for microcredit is 400 million people, and it's only now reaching 10 percent. All the microfinancing institutions in Kenya presently reach 120,000 borrowers and 200,000 savers, according to figures from the Central Bank. The market is estimated at 15 million people. The largest microfinancing institution, the к-Rep Bank, hopes to have 1 million customers by 2020.

Driving poverty from the world seems like a hopeless task. But the good news is that the success of the κ-Rep Bank is being imitated by the established banks. κ-Rep has already lost several staff members to established banks that want to turn their attention to microfinancing. The Cooperative Bank recently opened a branch next to the κ-Rep Bank in the Kawangware slum in Nairobi. In Bolivia, banks are showing television ads offering services to the lowest income groups. Indian banks make loans to women's groups in massive numbers.

This invasion of the established banks will enormously accelerate the spread of microcredit. The struggle against poverty will take time, but seldom has more success been booked than with the small-scale approach of microcredit and related policy. Prado of DAI in La Paz says, "This is the most important, most successful revolution that we could have brought here. And in Latin America that's saying something."

Padma

The purple alarm clock is ticking loudly – as if you could count the strokes of progress. Two tables with sewing machines betray the activity going on in the dark, stuffy workshop. On shelves along one side of the room are stacks of bright cotton fabrics, sorted like the colours of the rainbow. On the other side are small packages in the same colours. Packed in a kind of sticky cellophane are edgings for reinforcing saris. A curtain separates the space from another room which, like the first, is about eight metres square. It serves as the living room, bedroom and kitchen in one. The mud walls of the simple little house fail to block the smell of the outdoor latrine.

The sari-edging business owned by Padma and her husband, located in the village of Ilapuram in the Indian state of Andhra Pradesh, is two years old. She started with a loan of 30,000 rupees ($600 u.s.) from the Indian microfinancing institution basix. She needed the money to purchase fabric. The couple already had sewing machines, since Padma's husband was a tailor. Why the switch? Padma answers with a candid laugh, "We didn't make enough profit as tailors." The monthly net back then was 2,500 rupees ($50). The production of sari edgings has doubled it, making the repayment of the loan plus 24 percent interest no problem at all. Old debts have been paid, and Padma has no need of new credit from basix. Each quarter she takes the train and bus to Mumbai (Bombay) in the neighbouring state of Maharashtra to buy fabric, and she can pay for her purchases from the turnover.

The success of the business has already led to the hiring of an extra seamstress. Padma now works with her in production. Her husband no longer sits at a sewing machine but spends all his time selling their product. The annual income is now 200,000 rupees ($4,000 u.s.). Padma says the turnover in two years will grow to 550,000 rupees, which means more work for more people: three to four new jobs.

But that's not all. The seamstress is learning a new trade. The official from BASIX predicts that after this woman gets married she'll start up her own sari-edging business. "This is a typical effect that we observe in these kinds of small businesses," he says.

Padma's two daughters and one son go to a private school in the village. That costs 8,000 rupees ($175) a year, an investment in further progress. "My life is better than that of my parents," says Padma. Her father was a weaver. She is a businesswoman. The future is in her children's hands.

Behind the house, scrawny chickens are cackling in a whitewashed coop. Padma no longer has time for this side job. The coop is let to a neighbour.

CHAPTER 6

Take a Job or Make a Job?

Driving into the Ugandan capital of Kampala from the famous Entebbe airport – where Israeli commandos surprised dictator Idi Amin's forces to rescue hostages from a hijacked jetliner in 1976 – you see a remarkable industry in action. It's not a big factory with tall chimneys, but a series of workshops along the side of the road – some built around a single stone wall, others made of planks and sheets of scrap wood. These little open-air shops all manufacture iron fences: fences with sharp, menacing spikes; fences with round railings and square railings; stately black-lacquered fences with elegant gold knobs. If you need a fence in Kampala – or anywhere in Uganda – this is the place to get it. The only place.

But the extraordinary thing about the many tiny fence manufacturers is the absence of any kind of formal organization or rules. These workshops have no bookkeeping records. They're not registered with the local chamber of commerce. The electricity they use is often illegally tapped. There is no industrial union for the workers. They pay no taxes. But they do create fences for the citizens of Uganda – and they create jobs. This is the informal economy – the unregulated economy of microbusiness.

Estimates differ, but about half the economies in developing countries function as the Ugandan fence industry does: informally without regulations. In Kenya, employment in the formal sector has been declining for 15 years now. No official bus companies operate in Nairobi any more; all the transportation takes place in *matatas* – small buses run by independent, informal entrepreneurs who ride the route the bus lines used to take. No established industry exists, creating jobs. Almost all Kenyan school drop-outs find their futures in the informal economy. In 1976, two-thirds of the employed population of Venezuela worked in legal businesses; now that number is less than half. Only 10 percent of the population of Zambia has an official job. In 1996, Brazil reported a growth of 0.1 percent in the building sector, while cement sales during the first six months of that year rose by 20 percent. According to an analysis by Deutsche Morgan Grenfell, 60 to 70 percent of the building activities in Brazil are never recorded in the books. And only three percent of all new buildings are officially registered. For every 100 houses built in Peru, only 30 have legal permits; the other 70 fall into the informal sector.

In Bolivia, more than 100,000 school drop-outs "disappear" each year into the informal sector simply because there's no alternative. They may find work in the approximately 190,000 microbusinesses in the capital of La Paz and the sister city of El Alto. In those cities live more than a million people. An average family consists of five members, and that means practically every family in La Paz and El Alto runs a micro-enterprise. These Bolivians become entrepreneurs because there are no employers offering them jobs.

In other developing countries it's virtually the same story; According to the International Labour Organization (ILO), an agency of the UN, 85 percent of all jobs created in Latin America since 1990 have been in the informal sector. This includes everything from the mobile-telephone booths using cell phones, trash haulers, workshops that make knock-offs of brand-name goods, and even dentists who fill cavities without credentials. These activities don't count as official parts of the economy, but they play a large role in the daily lives and work of 80 percent of the world's population. Microbusinesses, most of them illegal, are the leading job makers in the developing world.

The vast majority of people are employees – job *takers*. Beside them is that rare breed – entrepreneurs, employers, job *makers* – who furnish work. Students are educated so they can get jobs later on in the labour market. Students learn how to apply for jobs. They don't learn how to transform their talents and skills into their own work.

This Western reality offers no prospects for the millions of poor in developing countries. In his book about founding the first micro-credit institution, India's Grameen Bank, *Banker to the Poor*, Muhammad Yunus writes, "I think the idea that a young person work hard in order to make himself useful to an employer is disgusting. It makes me think of the time when a young girl would learn from her mother how to make herself attractive for a young man so she could find a husband. A human life is too precious to waste it preparing to find an employer and then devoting one's entire existence to serving that employer."

It hasn't always been like that. A few hundred years ago there were no employers in Europe. Each person took his fate in his own hands and made his own work: farmer, carpenter, shepherd. The industrial revolution actually made entrepreneurs scarce in the West. The modern "entrepreneur" is often the manager of a company set up by someone else. In economic policy plans there's seldom room for the entrepreneur who makes his own work.

Similarly, the millions of small-scale entrepreneurs in poor countries don't play any role in the "official" fight against poverty. The governments of these countries – and of donor countries – aim for large-scale investments that are supposed to create the kind of work that eliminates poverty. It's a doomed policy (see the introduction), and the proof is the diminishing contribution of the formal sector in the economies of scores of developing countries. Economic policymakers invariably overlook the power inherent in the informal sector. The tragedy is that in their blindness to self-employment they pass up the greatest strength of any society: the creativity of its people.

If you start with creativity, the possibilities are endless. Yunus always counters the arguments of the preachers of doom who worry about rapid population growth in poor nations. "What's there to worry about? All those people eating and consuming? That's only taking one side into account. But these people produce, too. I see that people are creative. You've got to stimulate that creativity instead of worrying about population growth."

The paradox is that the creativity of people in developing countries is part of the "informal economy." The term alone suggests an offside position. John Kashangaki of k-Rep Advisory Services in Nairobi says, "The common idea is that the people in the informal sector are only busy surviving. Actually the informal sector is doing much better." A study by the Kashangaki consultancy and the Kenyan Central Bureau of Statistics, for example, shows that the average income of the approximately 1.3 million microbusinesses in the informal sector in Kenya is 2 1/2 times the legal minimum wage.

Anyone determined to fight poverty in Kenya must focus on those 1.3 million businesses. That's where the creativity and the spirit of enterprise are found. That's where the job makers are. Those businesses have a direct influence on the lives of millions of poor people, which is why they are deserving of attention and support. Only 10 percent of them have access to mainstream credit granted by financial institutions; consequently, only microcredit has any real meaning for fighting poverty in such a situation. The same is true for many other developing countries. Millions of entrepreneurs in thousands of villages worldwide are able to generate their own work, and thereby promote progress in their own surroundings. It's a winning recipe, with microcredit as the crucial ingredient.

This doesn't yet mean that there's an entrepreneur hiding in each and every poor person. Director Mahajan of basix says, "It's a mistake to think that all poor people want to be self-employed. Quite often they want to develop an activity of their own *in addition to* a safe and fixed salary, such as that of a farm worker. They buy a buffalo to bring in extra money." But Mahajan also sees the purchase of that buffalo as a first step in the direction of independent work – and that is the engine of progress. Nothing fights poverty more effectively than a continuous process of increasing value. After the first buffalo comes a second. That's the way the possessions – and the income – of poor people grow. And that growth occurs much faster through self-employment than salaried employment.

So the most hopeful prospect for progress and the fight against poverty lies in focussing on and stimulating self-employment – in the informal economy. The poor vendors who pounce on tourists in the big cities of the developing world are not the problem. They're the solution. The rising economic power of the developing countries is formed by millions of illegal, informal entrepreneurs. Informality is not an abuse that must be fought. It is increasingly becoming the norm. According to noted Peruvian economist Hernando de Soto, it's very much in governments' interests to integrate these representatives of the informal sector of job makers into the economy.

We meet Hernando De Soto in the prestigious Landmark Hotel opposite Marylebone Station in London, where he has been put up by his host, the Morgan Stanley investment bank. De Soto wrote the book *The Mystery of Capital*, which explores why capitalism has been such a success in Europe, North America and Japan but barely gets off the ground most other places.

A Dutch waiter serves tonic and nuts at a table with a starched white tablecloth. De Soto bends forward. "The West has a tendency to blame the people of the Third World. They accuse them of having too little drive and competence. I don't believe a word of it. I think it's an arrogant view. It's nonsense that unequal levels of prosperity in the West and the rest of the world can be explained culturally. The cities of the Third World are full of entrepreneurs. It's impossible to walk across a market in Asia or Latin America without encountering someone who wants to sell you something. Samuel Huntington [author of *The Clash of Civilizations*] is wrong. That view frustrates me. Poor people have just what it takes to make a profit out of practically nothing."

De Soto has come up with a remarkable explanation for the difference between poor and rich in the world: The rest of the developing world cannot profit from capitalism because of an inability to produce capital. And that has everything to do with the absence of legal structures and regulations. The developing world lacks the documents that underlie the success of capitalism.

It starts with a mortgage. In Western countries, a first or second mortgage on the entrepreneur's own house is often the most important source of financing for new enterprises. Every piece of land and every building in developed countries comes with a documentation of ownership. With that deed, property can serve as collateral that allows you to get credit. A poor entrepreneur in a developing country cannot use his assets in the same way to finance the growth of a business.

"The poor also own houses," says De Soto, "and those houses also have value. Even a rickety shack in a slum has value – your neighbour would be willing to pay for it. But that capital is dead because the ownership rights haven't been laid down. Without that formal registration, a bank won't give you a mortgage. The streets of developing countries are full of dead capital."

A random illustration: *Business Week* wrote that in 1995, four years after the fall of communism in the former Soviet Union, "two hundred eighty thousand of the 10 million farmers own their own land." De Soto and a team of students and staff from his Institute of Liberty and Democracy in Lima have been carrying out extensive land studies to determine the value of that dead capital. The team discovered that a hut in a slum of Port-au-Prince in Haiti would bring in $500 u.s., a shack along a polluted canal in Manila approximately $2,700, a respectable house outside Cairo $5,000, and a bungalow in the hills around Lima $20,000. On the basis of their research, the total value of non-registered real estate was estimated in Haiti ($5.2 billion), the Philippines ($133 billion), Egypt ($240 billion) and Peru ($74 billion). With that information, De Soto estimated the total value of all the properties in developing countries that cannot be used to create capital, and he came up with the incredible amount of $9.3 trillion – $7 trillion of which is in urban areas. "That's a low estimate. We based our figures on the replacement value of the real estate and not on the market value," he says. That $9,300,000,000,000 is an amount that stops you cold. It's equal to the total value of all the businesses listed on the most important stock exchanges in the 20 richest countries in the world. It's also more than 90 times all the development aid that all the industrialized countries together have given the developing world in the past 30 years.

Think what would happen if even a small portion of that inactive $9.3 trillion in capital owned by the poor of the world were brought into circulation. De Soto and his staff found that in developing countries today numerous informal regulations exist by which people protect their property rights. In Haiti – one of the poorest countries in the world, where more than half the population is illiterate – the owner of each parcel of land or shack has some sort of document he can use to defend his rights. "Wherever we looked," says De Soto, "most people in the informal sector had some kind of physical proof in which their property was put down."

The challenge is to create a legal and financial structure based on those documents that allows poor people to use their property as collateral for small loans.

De Soto makes a comparison with a mountain lake. You can fish in it and you can sail on it, but it doesn't produce very much that way. The value of the lake increases enormously if you build a hydro-electric power station under it. The falling water turns the turbines that generate electricity, which can provide power for new production taking place far away. Thanks to that mountain lake, the machines can run in a new factory.

That's exactly what would happen if that inactive $9.3 trillion were brought into circulation. In the West, money is brought into circulation almost exclusively on the basis of legal documents – such as mortgages. To put it simply, presidents of reserve banks control the flow of money in accordance with the number of new mortgages being registered. Bringing dead capital to life isn't a mission impossible. It's done all the time – beginning with the registration of real estate.

It sounds simpler than it is, though. The integrated ownership system on which the West relies and the financial world is based only came into existence within the past two centuries. In most countries, the system came about only 100 years ago, and in Japan about 50. Before then, the situation in the West was exactly as it is now in the developing world: A whole scale of informal ownership regulations existed. In the mid-19th century there were about 800 different ownership regulations in California alone.

A new waiter brings plates of pasta. The elite of London like to be served in an atmosphere of opulence. At a table nearby, an American businessman is talking a bit too loudly about his successes. De Soto hears it, too, and says assertively with an upraised finger, "A hundred years ago, America was a developing country. The sheriff was the clock. He decided how late it was in his area. And there were 700 different currencies. The pioneers who are applauded today by the Americans because they developed the land were pirates in their own time who broke all the rules."

Those pioneers were informal entrepreneurs, to use a modern phrase, who worked land that wasn't theirs. In 1783, George Washington spoke of "bandits who hold all authority in contempt while skimming off the land at the cost of many." At one point he considered dealing with colonists who had settled illegally on his own farm land in Virginia by having them forcibly removed. But more and more administrators and politicians recognized this as the road to disaster. The colonists would only come back the next day. (You see the same phenomenon in the slums of the developing world, where shacks are swept away by bulldozers one day and return in the same place or somewhere else the next day.)

In the United States, the chaos disappeared with the Homestead Act of 1862. Each colonist was given the right to 64 hectares (160 acres), provided he would live there and work the land. "This was no official gesture of generosity," says De Soto. "It was simply a recognition of the actual situation. Americans had already been occupying and working the land for dozens of years." After the Homestead Act came a series of other ownership acts that imposed uniformity on the informal situation. From then on, Americans could liquidate their legal property in order to make new investments. "That's how the Americans discovered the process by which they could create capital," says De Soto.

The law lags behind initiatives developed by the people. The challenge is to arrive at general legislation based on those initiatives. As the Romans wrote: It's all about *discovering* the law in existing customs and practises.

That's what De Soto did with his Institute of Liberty and Democracy in Peru, Egypt and Haiti, as well as other countries. At first he was very successful in Peru, his homeland, under President

Fujimori. The president gave him the freedom to replace old, complex, impenetrable systems and rules with simple, uniform regulations. Informal agreements were absorbed into the law and massive information campaigns were launched, calling informal entrepreneurs to have themselves registered. People complied in large numbers. "Entrepreneurs showed they were interested in legalization," says De Soto, "because they saw the credit possibilities. They immediately understood that banks did not want to mortgage their houses, but that they wanted to receive interest."

Three hundred thousand entrepreneurs registered. A million and a half existing buildings were given official deeds of ownership. A hundred twenty thousand new businesses were registered, 500,000 jobs created. In 1994, the economy of Peru booked the highest growth percentage in the world and continued this robust growth in the years that followed. Before De Soto got started, Peru accounted for 70 percent of the world's coca production. In 1994, that figure was down 25 percent, because farmers owned their fields and felt confident enough to invest in crops requiring longer cultivation. "Coca plants grow in six months. Palms for hearts of palm have a greater yield, but they grow in six years."

In the Netherlands it took 300 years before all the real estate was recorded in the land registry. De Soto did it in Peru in 10 years. But in 1995, the process ran aground with the fall of Fujimori. De Soto had to "pay" for his close connection to the discredited president. "I learned one thing: We shouldn't be identified with politicians who court the favour of the voter," he says in retrospect. In the meantime he has come a long way with his approach in Egypt and Haiti.

The formalizing process in the developing world can and must move faster than historic examples. Says De Soto: "It can be done in 10 to 15 years, and the first results will be booked after five years." In *The Mystery of Capital*, De Soto writes, "Eight million people were living in Great Britain when it began its 250-year trek from farm to laptop. Indonesia is making the same journey in only 40 years – with a population of 200 million. No wonder local institutions and regulations are slow to adapt. But adapt they must."

Further on he proves himself optimistic nonetheless: "The fundamental problem for non-Western countries is not the migration to the city as such, nor the accumulation of rubbish, the poor infrastructure or the emptying of the countryside. These things have taken place in Western countries, too. The growth of the cities isn't the problem either. Los Angeles grew faster during the 19th century than Calcutta did during the 20th, and Tokyo is three times bigger than Delhi. The primary problem is the failure to appreciate the fact that the chaos raging beyond the West is the consequence of a revolutionary movement that contains more promises than problems. As soon as the potential value of the movement is utilized, many of the problems will be easier to solve."

The challenge is enormous, and so are the possibilities. More and more heads of state and government leaders are coming to realize this. Hernando de Soto is an almost-permanent round-the-world traveller. He's spoken with Putin, Blair, Mubarak and Clinton, who apologized that their meeting was really "too late." Nigeria wants to start working with De Soto. So does Kazakhstan. And so does Ghana.

The day before our meeting, De Soto spoke with José María Aznar, the [former] Spanish prime minister. He asked him why Spain had *received* development aid until its entrance into the European Community (now the European Union) in 1979 and now *gives* development aid. Aznar replied that Spain had to adapt its laws so that it no longer mattered to businesspeople whether they did business in Madrid or in Oslo. By introducing order and logic to the Spanish bureaucracy and legal system, the foundation was laid for an enormous economic boost. That Spanish metamorphosis underscores the importance of good legal structures for a country's economic development.

"Most of what I say is about ownership because it's the easiest thing to understand," says De Soto, "but in the end it's all about a country's total legal structure." As an example he mentions a button manufacturer in one developing country. The buttons are first-class, but sales are in the hands of the brother of the entrepreneur's wife. And because that brother-in-law is no commercial genius, the little company never really breaks even. But no successful salesman wants to get involved in selling the buttons because he's afraid the entrepreneur will just copy his sales techniques and show him the door. So the entrepreneur is stuck with his incompetent brother-in-law – until he has his business formally registered. If he sets up a corporation and disburses shares, he can enter into partnerships. He can give or sell shares to the successful salesmen, who no longer need worry that their gimmicks will be copied. With this combination of talents the business grows quickly.

"Some people say you can't trust entrepreneurs in poor countries," says De Soto. "That's not the point. The trust we have in other people is often a result of agreements and regulations. If the customs official asks me, 'Who are you?' and I answer, 'I am Hernando de Soto and I was born in Lima on such-and-such a day and my mother's name is such-and-such,' he'll just give me an odd look. If I show him my passport, suddenly I'm somebody. He trusts that document. Or if the receptionist in a hotel asks me, 'How are you going to pay?' and I answer, 'Promptly,' that's not going to evoke a lot of trust. But if I take out my credit card, the problem is solved. I've got a portfolio full of documents that prove I'm someone who can be trusted within my particular environment. Eighty percent of the world's population doesn't have those documents. And when you're at Third World airports, do you know why you see so many boxes on the conveyor belts? It's because that's the most practical form of informal trade, necessitated by a lack of letters of credit and the like. Poor, illegal entrepreneurs lug around small quantities of products because they don't have the money to purchase in bulk, and because large quantities attract too much attention. A poor farmer brings his pig to market and another poor farmer wants to see the animal before he buys it. But traders who deal in quantities of pigs at the futures exchange in Chicago only trade on the basis of paper descriptions. They can trust those descriptions. They don't have to physically examine each animal. That's how large companies develop. In the Third World, legal limitations get in the way of

SMALL CHANGE

development. In short, successful enterprises require much more than the registration of real estate. But it is a crucial start."

De Soto is convinced that informal entrepreneurs would be only too glad to operate legally. There's no evidence that they choose illegality in order to avoid paying taxes. Because of the existing conditions, because of a lack of regulations, or regulations that are extremely complex and contradictory, there's often no alternative to illegality. De Soto's book is full of bizarre examples. It takes 289 six-hour working days to get a small enterprise registered in Lima. Registering a taxi takes six months. And it takes six years and 11 months to get permission to place a house on government land – involving 207 administrative steps and 52 government offices. In the Philippines, the same procedure, involving 168 steps and 53 government institutions, takes between 13 and 25 years.

Poor entrepreneurs would rather pay interest than be cut off from credit, and in the same way they regard the price of taxes as admission to the formal economy, with all its opportunities and possibilities. "The cost of illegality is high," says De Soto. "Transportation costs, for example. But inefficient collaboration with family members in the informal sector has a high price, too. No, faced with those expenses the poor would much rather pay taxes. Those taxes are not a drawback for entrepreneurs, and at the same time they're a source of income for the state."

So the ownership revolution that Hernando de Soto wants to launch has a wide range of beneficiaries. This mission has been propelling him for 20 years so far, and the moment of the big breakthrough seems to have arrived. But for De Soto, fulfilment doesn't come in the form of prizes or fame. He gets his satisfaction in the recognition of the vitality and creativity of what is somewhat disparagingly called the "developing world."

A cup of herb tea brings a moment of peace and quiet to the table. While De Soto pauses to prepare for a presentation to the fast-moving bankers of Morgan Stanley the next morning, my thoughts go back to the market woman I met in La Paz, who goes to Chile a few times a year by bus to purchase merchandise. "How do you carry it all?" I asked her. "In a box on the roof of the bus," she answered. One of De Soto's boxes.

Once again I appreciate the tremendous effort that illegal entrepreneurs put into keeping their small businesses afloat, like spending a few days in a bus to Chile a few times a year. Thanks to microcredit, the woman can buy more merchandise at once and bring back two boxes. Two boxes, more turnover, more profit so she can pay her children's school fees. De Soto is right: Poverty isn't a question of culture. The poor, illegal entrepreneurs may be the most enthusiastic, most creative entrepreneurs on earth. The Bolivian market woman and her millions of fellow job makers are waiting for politicians to pick up on De Soto's ownership revolution. As he says, "There's nothing better and more effective than this."

Jane

The customer in the chair, busily talking into her mobile phone, illustrates the success of this beauty parlour. The middle-aged woman, obviously well-to-do, comes from the centre of Nairobi, but for this morning's haircut she's come to the salon of Jane Gachucha in the Kawangware slum on the edge of the Kenyan capital city. Apparently Jane's beauty parlour is well-known outside the slum, and her prices are significantly lower than those of the downtown hairdressers.

In the salon, on the first floor of one of the few buildings with more than one story in Kawangware, are two hairdresser's chairs. The room is strikingly clean, perfume from a can of hairspray mixing with the stench of decay and sewage outside. Mirrors hang on the wall over a sink and shelves lined with hair products. On television, Senegal – "the pride of Africa" – is playing a game during the World Cup football championship.

Jane herself worked in a downtown beauty parlour until she decided to start her own business four years ago to provide more for her two children, adding to the income made by her husband, who has his own hardware shop. She bought her first hairdryer hood from savings. Next she invested in two more dryer hoods and two steam hoods with money from four loans from the Kenyan microfinancing bank K-Rep. Her first loan amounted to 15,000 shillings ($190 U.S.), at 18 percent annual interest, which she paid off in three months. Then there came loans of 20,000, 25,000 and 50,000 shillings. The value of the equipment in her salon doubled in four years – growth of 100 percent – to approximately $3,000.

At first Jane's salon was visited by an average of five customers a day. Now that's about 15, and she's hired two extra hairdressers – two more during December, the busiest month. Her daily turnover is now about 6,000 shillings ($75). "I regard myself as successful," says Jane confidently, "because I want to be." The success of her company has made it possible for Jane and her husband to buy a piece of land and to start building their own house for 1.5 million shillings ($19,000), without borrowing any money. In addition, her two sons of 11 and 7 recently switched from public to private school. The school costs 10,000 shillings ($100) a month, but the difference is considerable: The boys get breakfast and lunch at school, swimming, computer lessons and even German. "The sky's the limit," says Jane. "I want to do all I can to make their dreams come true."

Her next step is to open a hairdressers' school, where she plans to teach the hairdressers' trade to 15 students in courses that last six months and cost 30,000 shillings ($300). K-Rep is prepared to finance the establishment of the school. "It's my dream to be very rich," says Jane, first of all for her sons. After a pause, she says quietly, "I would also like to visit your country...and Australia."

People Before Profit

The successful advance of microfinancing in the past 20 years has run parallel with the advance of the market economy. Socialist ideals based on the presence of a powerful state had to make way for an even more powerful market. Governmental services were privatized. In the light of that development, it's tempting to regard microfinancing as "the privatization of the fight against poverty."

That view fits in with the prevailing free-market, liberal, international political and economic agenda. By this thinking, governments can stop subsidizing development programmes. Fighting poverty no longer requires money. Gifts and subsidies are replaced by loans; the poor finance their own development with their savings. That progress takes place first of all in small-scale terms in the immediate vicinity of the microcredit borrower, but ultimately it trickles down to the economy as a whole. Thanks to one small loan, the income of the poor entrepreneur increases and finally there's a demand for, say, a tube of toothpaste. A great many loans create a demand for a great many tubes of toothpaste. A market is created for a toothpaste factory. What began as a microcredit loan in the margins of the market expands to an engine of economic development in the broadest sense of the word. The free market solves the poverty problem.

Nice theory. But the reality of poverty and the gaping chasm between rich and poor is unmanageable. Mahajan of BASIX says, "We must not exaggerate the promises of microcredit and of the free market. More is needed than that. There are 300 million illiterates living in India. Southern Asia is the 'poverty capital' of the world, with 500 million people having to live on less than $1 a day. Those people cut down trees so they can cook their food. They undermine the environment on which they depend. The current organization of the free market doesn't provide water, trees and land. It's absolutely untrue that we can solve the poverty problem with credit alone!"

Microfinancing stimulates enterprise and economic development. That development issues from the free market and no longer requires traditional development aid. But in order to channel that progress, more is needed than the free market. Poor people don't only cut down trees for firewood. Peasants invest their loans in artificial fertilizer and insecticides, for instance, undermining a sustainable future for their land. The environmental factor plays no role as yet in microfinancing. "That's really the next step," says Marilou van Golstein Brouwers of the "green" Triodos Bank.

The struggle against child labour hasn't yet made its way onto the agenda either. In areas such as environment and child labour there's still a need for Western support and co-operation. Knowledge transfer is the key concept. That's why the pioneers of microfinancing see education as the main area to which rich countries and non-profit organizations can continue to direct their subsidies and gifts.

"Lack of good education is the source of all evil. Governments are too poor, so the salaries in schools are bad. Consequently schools are bad. So the children of the poor keep working as servants," says Prado of DAI in Bolivia. He points out that education is a typical subsidy area. "Education is subsidized in the rich Western world, too. In the West those subsidies come from tax monies. In developing countries, the subsidies still come from donor money – due to a lack of adequate tax income. Subsidies like these don't get in the way of economic development."

So full privatization of the fight against poverty is out of the question. Yet the success of microfinancing shows that capitalism can serve a much broader purpose than the reader of the daily stock market listings suspects. Sound enterprises in which *people, planet* and *profit* go hand-in-hand are now fashionable. Social and environmental objectives are linked to more traditional aims. That's a real achievement, but for the time being the pioneers of this progressive business community are most vocal in their insistence that sound enterprise does not have to come at the expense of profit.

Only a few dare acknowledge the unavoidable truth: Far-reaching investments in people (employees, customers, suppliers) and environment – investments that are necessary for a sustainable economy in the long run – must be made at the expense of shareholder profits. You cannot maximize profits and maximize service to people and nature at the same time. Sooner or later, a company will have to make a fundamental choice. Human beings and nature are of a different order than profit. The former are the goals of an enterprise; the latter is the means by which those goals are realized.

Microfinancing institutions, with their idealistic foundations, have taken the step to really sound enterprise. The leaders of this new movement are not to be found in the rich West but in the developing world. These institutions are succeeding in linking social and economic objectives, although they don't yet serve environmental interests. Profit is seen as a means to realize the social goals of the fight against poverty.

People come before profit. That's the vision of microfinancing institutions. Kimanthi Mutua of K-Rep speaks of the combination of "a gentle heart and a hard head." The social mission goes hand in hand with the pursuit of profit. "It's a creative tension that is necessary for innovation," he says. SHARE has still never lost a rupee in granting loans, and at the same time studies show that SHARE has been successful in fighting the poverty of its borrowers.

Ramirez, who turned the Bolivian FIE from a non-profit organization into a profitable microfinancing institution, puts it this way: "We want to safeguard our social mission. That's why we've been cautious in selecting our shareholders. They must be prepared to accept a lower return on their investment. If you fight poverty effectively it's really another form of profit."

Shareholders get lower returns. If they didn't, it would be at the expense of the goal of fighting poverty. Byarugaba of SOMED in Uganda says, "We want to do as much good as we can without taking a loss. We restrict our profits for the continuity of our organization." The one-sided struggle for maximized profits is replaced by a two-sided struggle for optimal social *and* economic welfare. That is capitalism with a human face at work.

Microfinancing institutions are fortunate in that there are shareholders prepared to be satisfied with lower returns in the interest of fighting poverty. At the moment, those shareholders are often idealistic institutions – such as international development banks – for whom lower yields are no problem. But Ramirez wants to go one step further with FIE: "Now most of our shareholders are in the West. My dream is that later on most of them will live in Bolivia." Ramirez is convinced that enough Bolivians are prepared to invest their money with lower returns if doing so would serve the progress of their country. Van Golstein Brouwers, who invests funds from the Triodos DOEN Foundation in FIE, supports that view: "Our financing is aimed at making ourselves superfluous. After about seven years they really shouldn't need us anymore."

Entrepreneurs who serve the community find investors willing to support their broader development goals. Microfinancing is an inspiring example of a new kind of capitalism in which people come before profit.

Andalu and Narasaih

Nakrekal is a weavers' village in the Indian state of Andhra Pradesh. "Birds of a feather flock together" is often the motto of markets in developing countries, but there's a special reason for Nakrekal's single-minded activity. The weaving machines make such a racket that other workers can't stand to be near them.

The walls of the houses in the rattling streets are whitewashed, marked along the lower sections with decorative terracotta bands. It makes for a well-cared-for effect. A recent welcome downpour has given the street a fresh look.

You can hear the rattling outside the house of Andalu and Narasaih, too. Inside, Narasaih is standing surrounded by four looms, his bare, sweaty paunch exposed. Andalu is folding fabrics. White fabric with beautiful golden edges is being woven on the looms – a total of 240 metres (790 feet) a day. This is the traditional fabric for *dhotis* and *saris*. Asked why the wrap he's wearing isn't made from his own fabric, Narasaih answers decisively, "*Dhotis* are for old men." Fashion is king, even in the poor Indian countryside. The fact that Andalu doesn't wear a white sari is easier to understand: Only widows wear white saris. White is the colour of mourning in India.

Andalu and Narasaih already had two looms when they learned about the microcredit institution BASIX. They used their first loan of 25,000 rupees ($500), plus 15,000 rupees in savings, to purchase two more machines. That investment increased their business's returns considerably. They had already invested in the connection to the electricity grid and in a machine that winds bobbins. Narasaih had become accustomed to the regular trip to the market for purchases and sales. And four looms can still be run by a single man.

The two weavers make 2,500 rupees a month profit ($50). That's much better than the salary of 1,500 rupees that Narasaih earned when he was still working for another weaver. This improvement benefits their three children, who can attend private school for 15,000 rupees a year. Even so, the future is not bright. The "old men" with *dhotis* are dying out, and no growth is expected in the widow market either. Four years ago a couple with four looms could still make 3,500 rupees profit. Narasaih would like to open a fabric shop, like the one owned by his brother-in-law. There doesn't seem to be a hole in the market there, either, but Narasaih is confident. "I can handle the competition," he says.

Acknowledgements

Without the hospitality, co-operation and openness I received from the founders of the microfinancing institutions I visited, this book could never have been prepared in such a short time. It was a little over six months between the first idea and the final publication. My heartfelt thanks go out to Kimanthi Mutua (K-Rep Bank), Benjamin Byarugaba (SOMED), Pilar Ramirez (FIE), Vijay Mahajan (BASIX) and Udaia Kumar (SHARE).

Chris Kasangaki – and his elderly Volkswagen bus in particular – played a vital role during my visit to Masindi, Uganda. Andrés Urquidi of FIE was a devoted source of support in La Paz, Bolivia. I never would have returned without "his" vaccination certificate. Every request I made to Vasundhari of BASIX in Hyderabad, India, was carried out faster than I could ask the question.

The Dutch microcredit pioneers of the Triodos Bank were present at the birth of the Dutch edition of *Small Change*, just as they continue to lead the way in Zeist when it comes to innovative financing and investing. Marilou van Golstein Brouwers in particular, who is dedicated to the worldwide introduction of microfinancing, was always ready with her vast knowledge, advice and assistance. Fred Matser and the Fred Foundation showed me the way to SOMED in Uganda, and then to examples of microfinancing in rural circumstances that I would never have experienced otherwise.

The conversations with publisher Jean Christophe Boele van Hensbroek of the Dutch press Lemniscaat resulted in important refinements and improvements. No other friend is better able to restrain my sometimes ungovernable enthusiasm with an all-revealing smile. I owe my thanks to final editor Tijn Boon for his meticulous care and his talent for combining precision with friendliness.

The *Ode* magazine team filled in the week-long gaps I left during the writing of this book, maintaining intense contact via telephone and e-mail. There's nothing micro about the credit they deserve.

Finally, this book was an extraordinary family undertaking. My daughter Majlie travelled with me to Kenya and Uganda. Devika accompanied me to Bolivia. These were incredible journeys of a proud father who hopes that the impressions gained will contribute something to the experiences of secondary school. All six of us travelled through India, where Nina and Wali played with the children of microcredit borrowers in the remote villages of the state of Andhra Pradesh. In Sri Lanka a significant part of each day during a three-week holiday was taken up in writing this book. Our happy and harmonious stay there was a source of inspiration for me and blurred the borders between living and working – a highly desirable thing.

Each chapter began with a conversation with my wife Hélène. Each chapter ended with reading her the text. Without that partnership in thinking and listening my fingers would never have found their way across my keyboard. The collaboration with her coloured my experience of writing this book. Together we hope that *Small Change* will help to increase the success of microcredit, bringing rich and poor closer together in this unequally divided world.

Microfinancing Institutions

I visited five institutions to write this book, in Kenya, Uganda, Bolivia and India. These institutions provide a representative picture of the development of microcredit and microfinancing in the Third World:

Fondo Financiero Privado (FIE)
Five women who were active in refugee work after the restoration of democracy in Bolivia – women without any financial background – set up the microcredit institution Centro de Fomento a Iniciativas Económicas (FIE) in La Paz in 1985, making FIE the pioneer of microcredit in Bolivia. Until 1998 FIE issued around 100,000 loans for a total amount of $70 million. In 1998 FIE was converted into a "private financial fund." Such funds fall under the supervision of the Bolivian banking supervisor and are allowed to manage savings. Since 1998 FIE has provided 97,000 people with $107 million in credit.

About 70 percent of FIE is owned by the non-profit organization from which the financial institution emerged. Other shareholders are the Swiss Development Corporation and ICCO.

Half of FIE is financed by savings and the other half by loans that have been granted by two Dutch institutions: the Triodos Foundation DOEN Fund and Oikocredit. In mid-2002 the credit portfolio amounted to more than $30 million, 7.7 percent of which is regarded as risky. The average loan now amounts to $1,211. In 1999 that was $1,014, and in 1998 it was $838. The total savings balance stands at more than $14 million.

The institution has about 24,000 credit customers and more than 1,000 savers. More than half the borrowers are female entrepreneurs with small-scale production and trading businesses: tailor shops, cobbler shops, textile companies, metalworking companies, vegetable operations, clothing businesses, etc.

In 2001, FIE booked a profit of almost 2.8 million bolivianos (almost $400,000).

The director of FIE is one of its founders, Pilar Ramirez, who also owns one percent of the shares. Ramirez received an award in 2000 from the Inter-American Development Bank for her pioneering work in Bolivia and for woman-friendly programmes in Latin America.

FIE
Casilla 15032
La Paz
Bolivia

Support Organization for Micro-Enterprises Development (SOMED)
SOMED began a volunteer programme for rural development set up in 1990 in Uganda by Benjamin Byarugaba. After reading an article about the Grameen Bank in Bangladesh, Byarugaba decided to launch a similar initiative in Uganda. SOMED began in 1998 as a Grameen clone with a gift of $50,000 U.S. from the Dutch Fred Foundation. This was followed by support from Hivos. SOMED's mission is "to grant small loans on a continuous basis to the disadvantaged poor, especially women, so they gain enough confidence to create prosperity that leads to fulfilling lives."

Ugandan law does not yet allow SOMED to manage savings, but a bill is now in parliament that will enable the establishment of small microcredit banks. SOMED hopes to become an autonomous institution in five years that will function without donor money.

With a total staff of 14, SOMED is active in the north of Uganda around the city of Masindi. It is a thinly populated area, which makes the costs high for every granted loan. SOMED now has about 5,000 borrowers who together have borrowed about 600 million shillings ($360,000). The average first loan for a SOMED customer

SMALL CHANGE

is $60 which is usually invested in vegetable stands, pulp cane-weaving companies, clothing dealers, cattle, etc.

SOMED
P.O. Box 3
Masindi
Uganda

Society for Helping and Awakening the
Rural Poor through Education (SHARE)
SHARE was established in 1992 by Udaia Kumar who came to the conclusion that technical-development programmes for poor people had no effect if the poor were not given access to credit at the same time. He was also inspired by the Grameen Bank in Bangladesh. In order to attract more funding, SHARE was converted into a profit-oriented microfinancing institution in 1999, a "non-banking financial company" registered with the Indian reserve bank.

SHARE, active in 1,700 villages in the Indian state of Andhra Pradesh, has a number of unique features. The company is owned by 26,041 of its borrowers. Since 1999, SHARE has issued loans to more than 115,000 people totalling 1.25 billion rupees (more than $25 million). All borrowers are women, and 85 percent of them are among the poorest of the poor in India. Two-thirds are illiterate. Nevertheless, SHARE has a 100 percent repayment score. Independent accountants have concluded that SHARE has never lost a single rupee in microcredit. The maximum first loan from SHARE is 4,000 rupees ($80). Customers are obliged to save a minimum of five rupees (10 cents U.S.) a week in a group fund.

Seven hundred people work at SHARE. In the fiscal year that ended on March 31, 2002, the company booked a profit of almost 4 million rupees ($80,000). Profits were also made in the two previous fiscal years, but so far no dividend has been issued.

The loans granted by SHARE are financed by loans from commercial banks and institutions. These include, besides a series of Indian banks, the Deutsche Bank and the Hivos Foundation-Triodos Fund and Oikocredit, of the Netherlands.

When SHARE has sufficient capital at its disposal, it will be permitted to manage savings as a registered financial institution.

SHARE
#1-224/58
Rajeev Nagar, Nacharam
Hyderabad 500076
India

BASIX

The Indian microfinancing institution BASIX was established in 1996 under the leadership of Vijay Mahajan. Mahajan had 15 years' experience in development work in rural India at the time. Earlier he had been the founder of the development organization PRADAN.

The objective of BASIX is "to promote a wide range of sustainable livelihoods for the rural poor and for women by means of financial services and technical support." BASIX strives to obtain "competitive results" for its investors in order to attract commercial capital on a continuous basis.

BASIX is made up of three organizations. First there is the "non-banking financial company" registered with the Indian reserve bank. This company is active in 3,100 villages in 19 districts in the Indian state of Andhra Pradesh. BASIX is also active in three districts of Andhra Pradesh as the first recognized Indian microfinancing bank allowed to manage savings. Finally, India Grameen Services functions as the non-profit organization within the BASIX group, providing technical support.

Since 1996, BASIX has granted loans totalling 745 million rupees ($15 million). BASIX has 32,000 customers in the countryside. A quarter of them are women. Half the borrowers consist of outcasts and other excluded groups. The average BASIX loan is 14,000 rupees ($280); 7.9 percent of the loans are more than 90 days overdue.

BASIX does not focus primarily on the poorest of the poor. According to the BASIX philosophy, the poorest Indians are helped more by working for entrepreneurs who are less poor than they than by being given loans to start their own businesses. From that point, with the knowledge they acquire, they can later become self-employed themselves.

BASIX shares are in the hands of the International Finance Corporation (IFC) in Washington, the Shorebank in Chicago and the Dutch Hivos Foundation-Triodos Fund, among others. Loans from the company are financed by commercial loans from mainly Indian banks. For the fiscal year ending on March 31, 2002, a profit was logged of more than 2 million rupees ($40,000).

BASIX
501-502 Nirmal Towers
Dwarakapuri Colony
Punjagutta
Hyderabad 500082
India

K-Rep Bank

The K-Rep Bank was formed in 1999 from the Kenyan Rural Enterprise Program, a development programme established in 1984, which provided technical support and pioneered the use of microcredit in Kenya. K-Rep was fully dependent on donor funding. That dependence frustrated the organization because policy had to be continually adjusted to satisfy the desires of the donors. In addition, K-Rep's activities became more and more focussed on the granting of microcredit. In 1994, K-Rep decided to become a specialized financial institution, but it took another five years before the institution could be fully recognized as a bank that could manage savings.

In the two and a half years as a bank, K-Rep has managed to take in 500 million shillings (more than $6 million) in savings from 30,000 poor savers. That money was used to grant loans to 16,000 people. The average loan is for $600. Savings have proven to be an extremely effective source for providing sustainable credit. By way of comparison: When it was still an informal microcredit institution between 1990 and 1999, the amount K-Rep collected from donors for issuing credit was 300 million shillings ($3.5 million).

κ-Rep Bank booked a profit of more than 42 million shillings (more than $500,000) in 2001. The shares of the bank are in the hands of Triodos Foundation-DOEN Fund, the African Development Bank and the Dutch Financing Company for Developing Countries.

κ-Rep
P.O. Box 25363
Nairobi
Kenya

Sources

David Bornstein: *The Price of a Dream: The Story of the Grameen Bank*, University of Chicago Press, 1997

Jayati Ghosh: *Women and Rural Finance* on "Frontline," May, 1998

Grameen Foundation USA: www.gfusa.org, Hege Gulli: *Microfinance and Poverty: Questioning Conventional Wisdom*, Inter-American Development Bank, 1998, Institute for Liberty and Democracy, The; www.ild.org.pe

Shahidur R. Khandker: *Fighting Poverty with Microcredit*, Oxford University Press, 1998

Joanna Ledgerwood: *Microfinance Handbook: An Institutional and Financial Perspective*, World Bank Publications, 1998

Vijay Mahajan: *Is Microcredit the Answer to Poverty Eradication?* BASIX, India, Microcredit Summit Campaign: www.microcreditsummitcampaign.org

Onze Wereld (the Dutch magazine *One World*), January 1999: special issue on microcredit

Opportunity International: www.opportunity.org, Mariá Otero and Elisabeth Rhyne (eds.): *The New World of Microenterprise Finance: Building Healthy Financial Institutions for the Poor*, Kumarian Press, 1994

Aminur Rahman: *Women and Microcredit in Rural Bangladesh: An Anthropologial Study of Grameen Bank Lending*, Westview Press, 1999

Kavaljit Singh: "Microcredit, Band-Aid or Wound?" *The Ecologist*, March/April 1997, p. 42

Hernando de Soto: *The Mystery of Capital: Why Capitalism Triumphs in the West and Fails Everywhere Else*, Basic Books, 2003

Muhammad Yunus: *Banker to the Poor: Micro-Lending and the Battle Against World Poverty*, Public Affairs, 2003

About the Author

Born in 1959, Jurriaan Kamp studied international law at the University of Leiden. He worked from 1979 to 1984 on the staff of the European Parliament, and from 1984 to 1986 as economics editor of the NRC *Handelsblad*, a leading Dutch newspaper. Between 1986 and 1990 he worked as a freelance correspondent in India for this newspaper as well as for the magazine *Elsevier* and for various broadcasting companies. From 1990 to 1993 he was chief economics editor of the NRC *Handelsblad*.

In 1994 Jurriaan Kamp and Hélène de Puy established the Ode publishing company, which issues a monthly magazine of which Kamp is the editor in chief. *Ode* is a current-affairs magazine that publishes the other face of the news. It reports on such issues as the abuses of free trade, doing responsible business, home schooling, the challenge of sustainable energy and the promising future of organic farming. *Ode* goes beyond the familiar dilemmas and searches for thinkers who ask new questions (for more information: www.odemagazine.com).

Ode also organizes meetings at which inspiring visions are shared within small and large groups. Kamp is co-initiator of the Treaty of Noordwijk aan Zee (December 2000), with signatories from around the world. This treaty contains basic principles for an economics in which people matter, not money and power.

Jurriaan Kamp has written other books published by the Dutch press Lemniscaat: *It Is Possible* (1998) and *Because People Matter* (2000). He frequently gives public lectures and presentations.

Jurriaan Kamp is married to Hélène de Puy; together, they have four children: Devika, Majlie, Nina and Wali.

COSIMO-ON-DEMAND
NEW YORK

COSIMO is an innovative publisher of books and publications that inspire, inform and engage readers worldwide. Our titles are drawn from a range of subjects including health, business, philosophy, history, science and sacred texts. We specialize in using print-on-demand technology (POD), making it possible to publish books for both general and specialized audiences and to keep books in print indefinitely. With POD technology new titles can reach their audiences faster and more efficiently than with traditional publishing.

> ➤ **Permanent Availability:** Our books & publications never go out-of-print.

> ➤ **Global Availability:** Our books are always available online at popular retailers and can be ordered from your favorite local bookstore.

COSIMO CLASSICS brings to life unique, rare, out-of-print classics representing subjects as diverse as *Alternative Health, Business and Economics, Eastern Philosophy, Personal Growth, Mythology, Philosophy, Sacred Texts, Science, Spirituality* and much more!

COSIMO-on-DEMAND publishes your books, publications and reports. If you are an Author, part of an Organization, or a Benefactor with a publishing project and would like to bring books back into print, publish new books fast and effectively, would like your publications, books, training guides, and conference reports to be made available to your members and wider audiences around the world, we can assist you with your publishing needs.

Visit our website at www.cosimobooks.com to learn more about Cosimo, browse our catalog, take part in surveys or campaigns, and sign-up for our newsletter.

And if you wish please drop us a line at info@cosimobooks.com. We look forward to hearing from you.

Printed in the United States
52622LVS00002B/46-144